MASTERS AT WORK

MASTERS AT WORK

BECOMING A YOGA INSTRUCTOR

ELIZABETH GREENWOOD

SIMON & SCHUSTER

New York   London   Toronto   Sydney   New Delhi

Simon & Schuster
1230 Avenue of the Americas
New York, NY 10020

First Simon & Schuster hardcover edition May 2019

SIMON & SCHUSTER and colophon are registered trademarks
of Simon & Schuster, Inc.

For information about special discounts for bulk purchases,
please contact Simon & Schuster Special Sales at 1-866-506-1949
or business@simonandschuster.com.

The Simon & Schuster Speakers Bureau can bring authors to your
live event. For more information or to book an event, contact the
Simon & Schuster Speakers Bureau at 1-866-248-3049
or visit our website at www.simonspeakers.com.

Manufactured in the United States of America

1 3 5 7 9 10 8 6 4 2

Library of Congress Cataloging-in-Publication Data

Names: Greenwood, Elizabeth, 1983- author.
Title: Becoming a yoga instructor / Elizabeth Greenwood.
Description: First Simon & Schuster hardcover edition. | New York : Simon &
Schuster, 2019. | Series: Masters at work
Identifiers: LCCN 2018049828 (print) | LCCN 2018053012 (ebook) |
ISBN 9781501199943 (Ebook) | ISBN 9781501199936 (hardcover)
Subjects: LCSH: Yoga teachers—Vocational guidance.
Classification: LCC RA781.67 (ebook) | LCC RA781.67 .G74 2019 (print) |
DDC 613.7/046—dc23
LC record available at https://lccn.loc.gov/2018049828

ISBN 978-1-5011-9993-6
ISBN 978-1-5011-9994-3 (ebook)

CONTENTS

BECOMING A
YOGA INSTRUCTOR

INTRODUCTION

The first time I encountered this thing called yoga was in the pages of my beloved *Seventeen* magazine at the end of the last century. I recall a photo spread of a rosy-cheeked teen in leggings and a tank top, assuming positions that seemed easy yet would provide covetable benefits: lying on the floor and pushing her thighs up into a small backbend to ease menstrual cramps and lower back pain, balancing on one foot while holding the other to improve concentration, even simply extending both arms out to the sides to strengthen and lengthen those muscles. As a mildly depressed and uncoordinated aspiring juvenile delinquent, team sports seemed lame to me. But these graceful exercises seemed doable. I practiced them on the carpet of my bedroom, and, whether due to a placebo effect or not, they felt good.

After a few weeks, I logged on to my America Online account via dial-up modem to check out the yoga classes in my midsized city in central Massachusetts. Zip. The closest offering was by a former dance instructor who taught Hatha yoga ("for strength and relaxation!" her website proclaimed) in her living room in a town thirty minutes away. The cost was $5 for sixty minutes. I begged my mom to drive me, and because I have a very good mom, she did.

Alongside a handful of suburban moms, I learned a flow of yoga poses recognizable to any beginner: downward dog, warriors one and two, tree pose . . . The forty- and fifty-something ladies found it funny that an angsty fifteen-year-old would be so into this gentle exercise. But in spite of the awkward tableau, something about the practice felt nothing short of magical. When I clambered back into my mom's car an hour later, I felt a subtle elation, a fuzzy warmth in my limbs, and a respite from the anxiety that so often plagued me. Now, looking back, I realize what was so special about yoga then, and what remains wondrous about the practice for me today, more than twenty years later: my body and my brain were in the same place at the same time.

Search #yoga on Instagram today and you'll see your screen awash in a sea of lean muscles, toned midriffs, and gams encased in neon leggings pressing up into an elegant handstand on a secluded beach. In the early twenty-first century, yoga has become synonymous with flexibility, radiant wellness, and perhaps a dash of levitating-above-it-all smugness. Yoga's ancient roots and its sheen of vague spirituality imbue the practice with gravitas you don't quite get, say, just lifting weights or shaking your booty in Zumba class. It's more than just exercise: it's a philosophy, an identity, a lifestyle.

But in spite of its image of impossibly healthy, green-juice-sipping, backbending exclusivity, yoga has never been more ubiquitous in the United States. A 2016 study[1] conducted by *Yoga Journal* and the nonprofit Yoga Alliance found that fifteen percent of Americans practice yoga—a whopping 36.7 million people—and seventy-two percent of those practitioners are women. Yogis practice at home, at the gym, and in studios, community centers, and parks. You can find a yoga class from Skokie to St. Petersburg, or peruse thousands of free instructional videos online. You can practice any number of novelty forms, including goat yoga, aerial yoga, beer yoga, chair yoga, yoga raves, hip-hop yoga, laughter yoga, tantrum yoga, and naked yoga. It's become a $16.8 billion industry.

Your average class at the gym might look something like

this: Yoga mats facing the front of the room. A teacher leading the class in a centering exercise, perhaps breathwork or a chorus of *om*s. She will demonstrate poses, beginning with a series of sun salutations, meant to raise body heat and energy. Perhaps the instructor walks around the class to make minor adjustments to forms, pulling back a hip here, dropping a shoulder there. You may hear a Sanskrit word or two— *namaskar A* or *virabhadrasana*. Once the body is warm and loose, students might drop to the floor to do deeper stretching: pigeon pose, perhaps, or backbends. The *ujjayi* breath— or oceanic inhale and exhale—leads the student from one pose to the next. Class will end with everyone's favorite, savasana, or corpse pose, where the class gets to retreat to kindergarten and lie on their mats with eyes closed.

In other words, our modern Western understanding of yoga centers on the asanas, or the poses we make with our body, and the deep breaths we take to bring our physical self and mind into union. But this emphasis on physicality is a relatively recent development in yoga's over two-thousand-year history. Training teachers to make yoga into a career is an even more recent development.

Fortunately, unlike a fashion model or a ballerina, you can become a yoga teacher at any point in your life. But how to begin? What questions should you ask yourself prior to enrolling in your first teacher training, and how do you choose the best one for you? What will you actually learn? And once you've invested time and money in your education, where do you go from there? How do you set yourself apart from the thousands of teachers who are certified every year?

In the following pages I will answer these questions and many more. But for now, let's start with some basics. Becoming a Registered Yoga Teacher requires two hundred hours of study in a training program certified by Yoga Alliance, the largest worldwide organization to audit yoga teachers and schools to be sure they're up to snuff. If you want to teach at a studio or a gym, graduating from one of these programs is essential. You can take your basic two-hundred-hour teacher training course as a monthlong retreat in Costa Rica or as a ten- to twelve-weekend program at your local studio. But wherever and however the training is offered, Yoga Alliance requires its certified programs to provide five areas of instruction: one hundred hours of techniques, training, and practice, which is where the bulk of asana work occurs; twenty-five hours of teaching methodology; twenty hours of anatomy and physiology; thirty hours of yoga philosophy, lifestyle, and ethics, which might include studying classic texts like the Bhagavad Gita and the Upanishads; and ten hours of practicum, where a student will lead classes of fellow students and give and receive feedback. The remaining fifteen hours are for the studio to disperse as it sees fit, according to its principles and emphasis. Some will allocate these hours to the business of being a yoga teacher or social media training. Toward the end of the program, participants should get the opportunity to teach community classes made of paying students to get some hands-on experience. The average cost of the training is around $3,000.[2]

Vinyasa and Hatha are the two most popular forms of yoga practiced in the United States today, and, unless you've opted to study at a lineage-specific school, such as Iyengar or Ashtanga, the techniques portion of your first teacher training will likely follow the principles of those schools. (Both include the familiar asanas and deep breathing, but while a Vinyasa flow is fairly fast-paced, Hatha holds each pose longer.) But beyond your first two-hundred-hour teacher training, a world of specialization awaits. Top teachers pursue their education ravenously, often taking several trainings or workshops a year. They seek out mentors—modern-day gurus—and wring as much wisdom and experience out of the seasoned yogis as possible. The learning never ends.

Loving your yoga practice is a good reason to start thinking about becoming an instructor, but all experienced teachers agree that love is only the beginning. What I came to learn after spending hours interviewing dozens of yoga teachers and taking their classes is that becoming a master is more like studying an art form than perfecting a trade. The Bhagavad Gita defines yoga as "skill in action." Teaching yoga means doubling down on those two elements.

In this book you'll hear from people who have approached yoga teaching as a second (or third or fourth) career, and as a first. You'll meet people who have stepped away from the security of full-time jobs to traipse the globe teaching on beaches or through YouTube, and those who lead one gratifying class a week while maintaining another occupation. You'll attend theory-filled classes with Abbie Galvin, a world-class instructor whom other yoga teachers gladly fly across the world to study with, and practice alongside newbies just starting out in their teaching careers, who are hustling like they've never hustled before.

In addition to guiding you through becoming a yoga instructor, this book will also illustrate the benefits of taking your yoga practice to the next level. Elevating your practice into a daily ritual can be transformational in ways that transcend the boundaries of a yoga mat. It's the practice of putting your body and brain in the same place at the same time, truly living in the moment—and experiencing that connection on a daily basis can be nothing short of revolutionary.

1

On a Friday morning in late winter, New Yorkers are fighting the remnants of yet another surprise storm. Trains are delayed, puddles of slush surpass ankles, and umbrellas flip inside out. Yet climbing up the narrow and uneven staircase to a second-floor yoga studio in a former factory building in the Bowery, a loft where Keith Richards once lived, the unpleasantness of the journey is alleviated by the arrival. Inside the airy space, a gray light filters in from three tall windows looking out onto a strip of boulevard, once home to drunks and derelicts, that today boasts athleisure boutiques, juice shops, an upscale organic grocery store, and this establishment, with a cheeky name to acknowledge its singularity: The Studio. What sets this space apart from the innumerable yoga studios in New York City is its unique offering, Katonah yoga, which draws on Taoism and Chinese medicine, and the advanced students who call this studio home. The Studio is, as its website proudly proclaims, "where your teacher comes to practice."

Despite the slush and snow outside, The Studio's main teaching salon is packed cheek by jowl with students and their requisite props. A basic Katonah setup includes a mat, two blankets, a long strap for adjustments, four blocks, and a cloth sandbag for weighing down various body parts. Several people have draped themselves over folding chairs in supported backbends, blocks under their heads and their limbs trussed up, a somewhat medieval-looking arrangement reminiscent of the rack. Other students cluster in small groups to laugh and catch up, creating an atmosphere that's more cocktail party than silent monastery.

Then Abbie Galvin enters the room. A petite sixty-three-year-old with a mop of curly brown hair highlighted with blond streaks, this unassuming yogini in Adidas wind pants and a white boatneck top is the reason the people in this room have braved the morning's gale-force winds. She got in late last night from a training in LA, where students traveled from as far as Europe to study with her. If she's tired or jet-lagged, she's not showing it.

Immediately she starts making adjustments, bringing another block for a fellow who's upside-down over a chair, and pointing students—many of whom are also Studio teaching staff—to where they can most usefully provide the many hands-on tweaks Katonah yoga is known for.

She notices a newbie, Margo, off in a corner in expensive leggings and a high ponytail—Abbie knows the hundreds of students who are regulars by name and face—and introduces herself. She asks Margo to sit with her feet together to create a diamond shape with her legs, and wraps a strap under her hips. Abbie is reading Margo's feet, which is something like a palm reading, except where lines might indicate your longevity (or lack thereof) or love life (or lack thereof), the crests and wrinkles of the feet correspond to strengths and weaknesses in the body and their correlative spiritual attributes. The practice comes out of Taoism, but Abbie has made the ancient technique pragmatic.

Abbie translates the lines of Margo's feet. By now, half a dozen students have gathered around. "See how the ball of the left foot is flatter than the fullness of the ball of the right foot? That means the left lung isn't getting enough air," Abbie says. The flatness is the result of a dip in Margo's hip, itself the product of her organs being "collapsed," as Abbie terms it, or not functioning at their optimal capacities.

"Ah, that makes sense," says one of Abbie's disciples.

"Of course it makes sense," Abbie jokes. "I'm a person who makes sense!" Her teaching style is more brassy Borscht Belt Joan Rivers than guru en route to nirvana.

Abbie continues diagnosing newbie Margo by placing a tiny foot on her sternum. The woman grows several inches: "Now *this* is how you plug in, how you rise up, how you put yourself in the center of yourself."

"Wow, it feels so awkward," Margo observes.

"Everyone is off-center," Abbie tells her, along with the several students who are now taking notes. "It's not pejorative. If something is wrong, it's just because you don't know. Now you've got lungs, a socket, an antenna," she says, using the metaphor-heavy language of Katonah. "You're plugged in. Your job is to reference this idea, instead of just doing you."

Whereas many yoga teachers will urge students to "listen to their bodies" to find shapes that feel right to them, Katonah stresses objective measurement, using props like blocks and straps to ensure limbs land where they are supposed to. "Freedom is not doing whatever the fuck you want," Abbie says. "It's about finding freedom within confinement. It's about having good boundaries."

This is all before class has officially begun.

———

UNLIKE MOST CLASSES, WHERE yogis line up their mats to face the teacher at the front of the room, Katonah students place their mats to face the center. The configuration creates a more communal experience, and Abbie is rarely in one spot for longer than a minute. She commences with a pose recognizable to any lay student of yoga. "Let's get into a dog," she says, and the room suddenly quiets. "It's not the most interesting pose," she acknowledges with a laugh. "Now get your ass way up!" I giggle. "Now look way out," she continues. "That's the way toward your future. Would you rather look at your crotch or into your future?"

Abbie guides us into a modified cat-cow stretch, a gentle undulation of the spinal column. But things get interesting when she asks us to cross our legs behind, and to begin flipping our wrists to "move currency" through the body. "Beautiful, Jonathan!" she shouts across the room to a fellow whose body type is more plumber than yogi. "So nice, Alex!" admiring the form of a Studio teacher with triceps sharp like knives.

In Abbie's classes, students hold poses for much longer than the typical few breaths, although Abbie would likely quibble with my phrasing. "You don't *hold* poses," I hear her explain from across the room. "You move currency through forms. You orient yourself." She urges us to find the balance between exertion and punishment: "You don't drive until you run out of gas; you drive until you reach your destination."

In a particularly pretzely forward fold, where we swim our arms to grab opposite ankles, a regular, Harry, shouts, "This is hard!"

"Life is hard," Abbie claps back. "You could look a little happier!" Toward the end of class, she tells us to bring our mats to the wall to use the hard surface behind us as leverage to go deeper into a lunge known as pigeon pose. "But don't take all day!" she shouts with a smile as we find ourselves new spots. The laughter breaks through the sound of weary breathing.

Abbie's gift is seeing the wonkiness that resides in all bodies. She can spot a wrinkle in the neck or a torqued hip from across the room. She often demonstrates proper alignment on individuals, wrapping her ubiquitous strap around a waist and placing a foot into the crook of a hip to magically imbue the person with more inches and internal space, as a small cabal of teachers and seasoned students forms around her to watch. At one point, she walked all 105 pounds of her body up a gentleman's back. Her classes are more of a workshop than a traditional flow, and devotees come not only to work up a sweat but to gain knowledge of her philosophy, both in theory and in how it manifests in the body.

Abbie's microscopic attention to detail cuts both ways. Toward the class's close, she readies us for King of the Mountain, a pose where you interlace your fingers, palms

King of the Mountain Pose

up, and hold your arms above your head for a full nine minutes with a yoga block balancing on your palms, "your crown." I urge you to attempt this for thirty seconds. My arms go tingly in under a minute.

"Liz, you have trouble keeping your arms up, right?" she shouts to me in the farthest corner of the room, where I've sought refuge in an attempt to hide myself from the teacher-students and their circus-like contortions. My face flushes guiltily. I've been practicing yoga off and on for twenty years, and like to think I know a thing or two.

She calls me over to stand against a wall, where she places three blocks behind my upper, middle, and lower back, and one between my thighs. She has another student put a block behind my head while she lies on her back driving her feet into my hips. All thirty-odd students in the class are staring at me as Abbie points out my asymmetries and the fruitless angle at which I was attempting to hold up my arms without the scaffolding she has built around me. I feel a mustache of perspiration forming on my upper lip. "Straighten your arms," she urges me. She's narrating for the class now: "Her lungs are starting to fill, and she'll be able to start breathing. That's it, right! That's where she belongs."

After all the blocks and feet and straps have guided me into the position in which the pose is meant to be assumed,

I find I can hold my arms up effortlessly for the entire nine minutes. I feel that elusive currency I've heard her mention coursing through my body, as though for the first time all the organs and muscles of my body are conspiring to help rather than hurt me. When I release my arms back to their sides and shake out my legs, I feel a new lightness, a flush of energy. I can see why people get addicted to this kind of yoga.

2

I sometimes think how odd it is that both a mastiff and a Chihuahua can be called "dogs." The same holds true for Abbie Galvin's bespoke Katonah style, whatever Vinyasa flow you've been doing at the gym, and yoga as practiced in India four and a half thousand years ago.

Yoga derives from the Sanskrit word *yuj*, meaning "to unite" or "to join," in the way one would hitch an animal to a wagon (similar to *yoke*). The metaphor is about connection—the individual deriving power from a greater source outside oneself. The word comes from Sanskrit speakers of the Bronze Age who were migrating from modern-day Russia to the Indian subcontinent via the Indus Valley, circa 2500 BCE. Most of the yogic traditions of this era were transmitted orally—the highest teachings kept secret intentionally—and what was written down comes to us mostly through religious texts. The Rig Veda (circa 1500 BCE), a collection of hymns and one of the four canonical Hindu texts, depicts warriors practicing yoga prior to battle. The Bhagavad Gita, written sometime between 500 and 200 BCE, depicts a dialogue between the warrior Arjuna and his charioteer, Krishna, who reveals himself to be the Supreme Lord. Krishna lays out three paths of yoga through which the student can come to know his salvation. These include the path of action, or karma yoga; devotion, or bhakti yoga; and knowledge, jnana yoga. While the Bhagavad Gita mentions several modern-sounding yoga practices, such as breath control, this was intended for "withdrawal of the senses"—to receive strength from a higher power—rather than mind-body balance. Self-realization was the ultimate goal, with practice likely reserved for a rarefied group of holy men in the noble Brahmin caste.

The *Yoga Sutras*, 196 aphorisms on the theory and practice of yoga, was written circa 400 BCE and compiled by the author Patanjali. Little is known about his life, or if he is even a single individual. But his legacy is unparalleled. The *Yoga Sutras* are widely considered the ur-text of classical yoga, referred to as *raja*, or "royal" yoga, with philosophical roots not only in Hinduism, but also in Buddhism, Jainism, and other ascetic traditions of the Indian subcontinent of the era. The sutras lay out yoga as a system of living, the eight limbs (or elements) of this system being the *yamas*, moral imperatives such as nonviolence and truthfulness; *niyama*, virtuous habits and behaviors; *asana*, posture; *pranayama*, breath control; *pratyahara*, withdrawal of the senses; *dharana*, concentration; *dhyana*, contemplation; and finally *samadhi*, oneness. But while the word *asana* appears here as the third limb of yoga, it is defined not as the cycle of poses we think of today but merely as the position of the body that sets you up for seated meditation practice. The biggest difference between ancient and modern yoga is the emphasis on physicality. For thousands of years yoga was more synonymous with long sessions of stationary meditation than with exercise.

An important outgrowth of the *Yoga Sutras* was Tantra, which for the first time looked to the physical body as the route to enlightenment, aiming to awaken dormant energies. Tantra broke with the belief that there is a separation between the material and spiritual worlds; rather, the practitioner of Tantra can break down binaries such as pain and pleasure, or male and female, because all is contained in the universal consciousness. Everything is divine. This democratic worldview was reflected in the wide array of people who practiced Tantra: men as well as women, laypeople and nobles alike.

Hatha yoga evolved in part out of Tantra, with the teachings of *hatha* (meaning "sun" and "moon") attempting to integrate the panoply of yoga systems that had sprung up across the subcontinent and urging the yogi to "traverse a path toward a goal."[3] The fifteenth-century *Hatha Yoga Pradipika* lays out a system of asanas that would be familiar to a yoga student today, including *virasana* (hero pose), *gomukhasana* (cow face pose), and *savasana* (corpse pose). Accompanying purification rituals were meant to ready the human body to commune with higher powers. Some of these practices are still familiar, such as *neti*, or cleansing of the nasal passages with water, which has become a recommended treatment for sinus problems, and *mudras*, gestures meant to balance the energetic channels of the body, which you might see your teacher demonstrate by placing thumb and forefinger together during seated meditation. Rituals you likely won't see at your yoga studio include *dhauti*, which entails cleansing the stomach by swallowing a long piece of cloth, and *basti*, a yoga enema where one sucks water into the colon by creating an abdominal vacuum.

Hatha was practiced in India until the colonial era, when the postural shapes of lotus and backbending became associated with a British disdain for the "backwardness" of wandering yogis. As Mark Singleton writes in *Yoga*

Body,[4] his seminal history of physical yoga practice, "The emergence of the yogi as panhandling entertainer was a response to the uncompromising British clampdown on ascetic trade soldiers from the nineteenth century onward." British colonists and Christian missionaries saw Hatha yoga as savage.

But as yoga was being dismissed by outsiders in India, it was becoming an object of fascination elsewhere in the world. In 1842, three Harvard alumni formed the American Oriental Society, which hoped to study a vastly defined swath of land they deemed "the Orient," from Egypt to Japan. This "new" field of study was very much in vogue, and language and translation were essential to the endeavor.

The ability to disseminate Sanskrit texts in English made a big impact on the American Transcendentalist movement, which was then taking root in Harvard's backyard. In 1843, Ralph Waldo Emerson read the first English translation of the Bhagavad Gita, which Henry David Thoreau would reference reading in *Walden* as part of his daily routine during his monastic experiment. Thoreau's ascetic existence of contemplation at Walden Pond was also profoundly influenced by H. H. Wilson's *Sketch of the Religious Sects of the Hindus*, in which Wilson describes a state of meditation wherein "the Yogi is liberated in his living body from the clog of material incumbrance [sic], and acquires an entire command over all worldly substance."5 Thoreau's soon-to-be-famous book was published in 1854, and three years later, Emerson would publish a poem called "Brahma" in the first issue of the *Atlantic Monthly*, exposing Americans to "exotic" Eastern philosophies. Even before the Civil War, yoga was showing up in pop culture.

Two decades later, in 1875, the Theosophical Society was established in New York City. Its members dealt in a mélange of Hindu and Buddhist philosophy and a smattering of astral projection, telekinesis, and clairvoyance. Through this group, well-to-do New Yorkers were first introduced to the concepts of karma and nirvana. They were wowed by the reported magical abilities certain yogis possessed, seemingly manipulating the planes of time and space, "over men and natural phenomena," as the *New York Times* wrote in 1889. The society splintered into factions that championed either Raja yoga, mostly meditation and breathwork, or Hatha, which was associated with trickery and the body. Either way, their interest was more along the lines of intellectual pursuit than physical practice.

Few Americans, not even members of the Theosophical Society, would meet a yogi in the flesh until the Chicago World's Fair of 1893, the great feat showcasing modern technology and culture of the time. Held in honor of the four hundredth anniversary of Columbus's arrival in North America, the six-month-long exposition featured marvels that symbolized the United States' prowess in industrial and technological advancement. One of the most spectacular events was the Parliament of the World's Religions, marking the first interfaith dialogue between Eastern and Western spiritual traditions. The most captivating speaker was a Hindu monk, Swami Vivekananda.

Born in 1863 to an affluent Bengali family in Calcutta (his father was a successful attorney), Vivekananda's interest in spirituality began early; he is said to have meditated before images of the gods Shiva and Rama from a young age. Lore has it that the boy, insatiably curious, sought out spiritual leaders of all backgrounds to ask them a single question: Have you seen God? When he put this question to Sri Ramakrishna, the influential Hindu mystic and yogi at the Dakshineswar Kali Temple, Ramakrishna is said to have replied, "Yes, I have. I see God as clearly as I see you, only in a much deeper sense." This response enticed Vivekananda, and he went to train with the guru, taking his monastic vows in 1886.

Most point to Swami Vivekananda's stateside arrival as the moment yogic concepts were widely introduced to the

West. On September 11, 1893, he took the stage before an audience of seven thousand to kick off the Parliament of the World's Religions. He bowed to Saraswati, the Hindu goddess of learning, and then kicked off a barn burner of a speech. "Sisters and brothers of America!" he addressed the teeming crowd. Reports say he got a two-minute standing ovation at these words alone. "I thank you in the name of the mother of all religions, and I thank you in the name of the millions and millions of Hindu people of all classes and sects," he continued.[6] His speech went on to tout the values of universal acceptance and tolerance, and quoted the Bhagavad Gita. Schoolchildren in India still memorize the speech today.[7]

The swami was a sensation. Press accounts called him "the cyclonic monk from India" and the *New York Critique* breathlessly reported, "He is an orator by divine right, and his strong, intelligent face in its picturesque setting of yellow and orange was hardly less interesting than those earnest words, and the rich, rhythmical utterance he gave them."[8] An overnight celebrity, he became known as "the handsome Oriental," for his soulful eyes and brilliant orange turban. In his last speech to the Parliament of the World's Religions on September 27, he intoned: "The Christian is not to become a Hindu or a Buddhist, nor a Hindu or a Buddhist to become a Christian. But each must assimilate the spirit of the others and yet preserve his individuality and grow according to his own law of growth." Americans were certainly keen to assimilate the yogic practices of the swami. Due to popular demand, Vivekananda stayed in the United States for a few years afterward. He lectured at Harvard in 1896, where Radcliffe student Gertrude Stein heard him speak. He so impressed the eminences of the institution that they offered him the position of chair of the Eastern philosophy department. He declined, already saddled with his monastic duties.

Although Vivekananda is widely cited as importing yoga to the US, he was passionately against the Hatha yoga most Americans practice today. He had come of age in a colonial India where the physical aspects of yoga got lumped in with occultism and fortune-telling. Yogis who practiced Hatha yoga were considered diabolical, even by their peers in other yogic sects. Others conflated yoga postures with the sexual positions of the *Kama Sutra*, the first English translation of which appeared in 1883. The link between asanas and degeneracy was cemented in the minds of many, including Vivekananda.

In his 1896 book *Raja Yoga*, Vivekananda dismisses Hatha yoga, writing, "We have nothing to do with it here, because its practices are very difficult, and cannot be learned in a day, and, after all, do not lead to much spiritual growth." His goal for practitioners was transcendence through meditation rather than base physical development. In a talk he gave in San Francisco in 1900, he lambasted the principles of Hatha yoga further: "There are some sects called Hatha-Yogis . . . They say the greatest good is to keep the body from dying . . . Their whole process is clinging to the body. Twelve years training! And they begin with little children, otherwise it is impossible!"[9] To Vivekananda, the body was more of an impediment to the spirit rather than an entity unto itself to condition and celebrate. (It may be worth noting that Vivekananda would die just two years later at the age of thirty-nine.)

Swami Vivekananda wasn't the only yogi to land in America during the last decade of the nineteenth century. He was soon followed by Swami Abhedananda, who had also studied under Ramakrishna. Vivekananda sent his fellow guru to America in 1897, where he became the resident swami at the recently founded Vedanta Society of New York. Swami Abhedananda did not share Vivekananda's disdain for Hatha yoga. He guided his students through the basics of asana and pranayama practice, believing them to be quite beneficial to "unawakened souls" with no understanding of the breadth and scope of yoga. He was right. In 1900, the *New York Herald* published an article about a new trend preoccupying upper-class New Yorkers: "There are scores of men and women, perhaps hundreds, well known in New York's fashionable circles, who have taken up Yoga in their ceaseless efforts to do something . . . You might see my lady, clad in the loosest of flowing robes, sitting on the floor for hours at a time in some ridiculous posture, gazing at the tip of her nose."[10] By 1907, there were six chapters of the Vedanta Society in the United States, in Manhattan; Brooklyn; Washington, D.C.; San Francisco; Los Angeles; and Santa Clara County.[11] There was also the Green Acre center in Maine, the model for the yoga retreats still popular today.

The yoga the *Herald* sends up still hews fairly close to the meditative practices Vivekananda championed. But in the late nineteenth and early twentieth centuries, a renaissance in athleticism was emerging in the UK, Europe, and the United States. Industrialization was changing society, and many worried that men were becoming too "soft." In the United States, swaggering fellows such as Theodore Roosevelt warned that the creature comforts of cities and mass production would be the downfall of the country. He famously declared, "The things that will destroy America are prosperity at any price, peace at any price, safety first instead of duty first, and love of soft living and the get-rich-quick theory of life." The antidote to such decadence was exercising the body, a means of demonstrating not only the strength but also the character of the nation.

It would be the Young Men's Christian Association, or YMCA, seen today across the world as an anodyne gym, which would make physical culture a readily consumable commodity. Founded in London in 1844 and soon exported to the far reaches of the British Empire, the organization was a response to the "unhealthy" social conditions arising in big cities at the tail end of the Industrial Revolution. In Indian YMCAs, physical culture gained a sort of moral respect, a status it had not previously enjoyed. Pennsylvania-born Harry Crowe Buck, who founded the YMCA College of Physical Education in Madras (modern-day Chennai), reported that he was "constantly searching for attractive indigenous activities which are suitable for physical education,"[12] in an attempt to combat the colonial stereotype of the "effete" Indian. The yoga asanas advanced at the YMCA were more muscular and utilized for bodybuilding than ever before. Whitewashed of their mystical connotations, yoga asanas became a core component of physical education.

A steady stream of Indian yogis, now more practiced in and accepting of the physical branch of yoga, continued to trickle into the United States until 1917, when union leaders in California got Congress to pass a bill keeping Indians and other Asians from settling in the US. These quotas stayed in effect until 1965. In the meantime, if Americans wanted to learn yoga, they had to go to India to do so. One such person was Indra Devi, née Eugenie V. Peterson.

Born in Riga, Latvia (part of the Russian Empire at the time), in 1899, Devi trained at a drama school in Moscow. In 1917, she fled from the Bolsheviks to Berlin, where she became an actress and dancer. Her fascination with India started early, when she encountered a yoga instruction book at age fifteen. When she was twenty-eight, she lit out for the subcontinent, adopting her Hindu-sounding name to act in Indian films. She met her Czechoslovakian attaché husband in Bombay (now Mumbai). They married in 1930, and through him she became acquainted with the maharaja and maharani (the equivalent of a provincial king and queen) of Mysore, who maintained a yoga school. The principal teacher was Sri Tirumalai Krishnamacharya, whose athletic asana sequences helped shape modern-day Vinyasa practice. Despite his initial resistance to teaching a Western woman, he became her guru. Her fellow students included K. Pattabhi Jois and B. K. S. Iyengar, who would go on to spearhead Ashtanga and Iyengar yoga, respectively.

In 1939 Devi's husband was transferred to China, and he urged his wife to open a yoga school in Shanghai. She did, and Madame Chiang Kai-shek became one of her students. Devi returned to India after World War II, where she penned *Yoga: The Art of Reaching Health and Happiness*,[13] the first book on yoga authored by a Westerner to be published in the country. She became the first Western woman to teach yoga in India.

After her husband's death in 1946, she moved to America the following year and opened a yoga school in Hollywood, where movie stars such as Greta Garbo and Gloria Swanson were regulars. Devi's physical translation of yoga met the needs of starlets seeking to "reduce." She also befriended cosmetics entrepreneur Elizabeth Arden, who incorporated yoga into her popular health spa programs. In the same way celebrities and so-called influencers put trends on the map today, so too was this true in the 1940s, when Americans began looking to Hollywood for aspirational fitness regimens.

The midcentury yoga craze didn't just touch actresses desperately seeking a fountain of youth. Writers Aldous Huxley (best remembered for *Brave New World*) and Christopher Isherwood (whose *The Berlin Stories* was the basis for the musical *Cabaret*) were members of the Vedanta center in the Hollywood Hills, founded by Swami Prabhavananda. Isherwood collaborated with the swami to issue a new translation of the Bhagavad Gita in 1945, which *Time* called "a distinguished literary work . . . [that] may help U.S. readers understand not only the Gita itself, but also its influence on American letters through one of its greatest U.S. admirers, Ralph Waldo Emerson."[14] Isherwood and Prabhavananda went on to publish three original books on yoga, all of which sold robustly. Huxley's *The Doors of Perception* and *Island* include unmistakable references to yogic ideas such as Tantra.

But it was the American yoga teacher Richard Hittleman who brought yoga out of the elite cultural enclaves and delivered its wisdom to the masses. Hittleman studied in India under the spiritual master Ramana Maharshi. Returning to the United States in 1950, he soon published the first of a number of easy-to-follow guidebooks that sold millions of copies.[15] His 1961 television show, *Yoga for Health*, influenced the way yoga has been taught in the United States ever since: somewhat divorced from its spiritual origins, with a relatable teacher in workout clothes (no bearded guru with flowing robes) showing asanas that are similar to calisthenics. This yoga was all about exercise. Hittleman would go on to open his self-described "largest full-time Yoga

College in the U.S.A."[16] in New York before the decade's end. Now, thanks to Hittleman, there would be a place to train yoga teachers domestically.

Many Americans had some grounding in the principles of alignment and meditation when 1968 rolled around, which *Life* declared "the Year of the Guru." The Beatles had taken up with Maharishi Mahesh Yogi, the founder of Transcendental Meditation. And though the maharishi did away with many aspects of yoga to focus on straight-forward concentration exercises to help the student achieve a state of bliss, most Americans weren't attuned to these variations in practice. Images of the Beatles and Mia Farrow in traditional Indian dress with garlands of mari-golds were enough to give yoga countercultural cachet. With this new youthful allure, and with the immigration quotas of the 1910s and 1920s recently reversed, a wave of teachers emigrated from India to the United States, many of them forgoing the traditional intimate relation-ship between guru and student to cannily market their ex-pertise for a consumer-obsessed culture. One such guru, Swami Satchidananda, eventually opened thirty branches of his Integral Yoga Institute—essentially making himself a franchise—and famously led the opening invocation at Woodstock in 1969.

As yoga historian Stefanie Syman writes in *The Subtle Body*, "By 1969, yoga was something the hippies had in common with their putative enemies: the middle-class conformist, the corporate drone, the happy housewife."[17] Yoga had reached critical mass.

3

Abbie Galvin was first introduced to yoga as a freshman at Barnard, when a boyfriend brought her a few hours upstate to the brand-new Sivananda Ashram Yoga Ranch in the Catskill Mountains. Established in 1974, disciples of the late Swami Sivananda taught a series of asanas based on classical postures for health and fitness. Swami Sivananda himself had been influenced by the famous yogi Bishnu Ghosh, who had been instrumental in developing the kind of muscular physicality we associate with yoga today. The sequence Sivananda codified and perfected, like others taught by future gurus who would splash onto American shores, is one made to be followed to the T, without improvisation.

Abbie had a hard time connecting to the practice's rote repetition of poses, despite the fact that yoga was wildly in vogue at the time. "I found nothing to hook into in terms of real theory," she tells me over tea in The Studio's kitchen, a comfy gathering place for students and teachers to chat between classes. "It was very devotional, more about reciting things rather than getting a real understanding of the principles or exploring ideas. I couldn't find an emotional or intellectual portal in. I loved the physicality of yoga, but I couldn't understand why I was doing it." She laughs. "Also, there were a lot of Americans from Ohio pretending to be Indian, and that kind of turned me off."

The road to becoming one of the most sought-after yoga teachers in the world was not a straight one. Abbie didn't even begin studying yoga seriously until she was in her late thirties. But she had spent her entire life as a student. And more than that, as a talker—an essential quality for any yoga teacher, for whom putting shapes and feelings into words is a prerequisite.

Abbie and her twin sister, Carol, were born in Chicago in 1955, and, according to their physician father, were in the womb facing each other and communicating from day one. "We were a world unto ourselves," Abbie says.

The girls were born into a family that used their voices. Their father was a gifted vocalist, and sang opera for extra food as a young boy on the boat from Poland when he immigrated to the United States. Abbie believes he could have rivaled Luciano Pavarotti, were it not for the first-generation pressures upon him to become a doctor. Abbie's other sister, Leslie, is a cantor. Her daughter is a voice-over actress, her youngest son is an actor (he performed on Broadway as the lead in *Dear Evan Hansen*), and her eldest son is the lead singer of the rock band Yoke Lore.

Study and inquiry were fundamental to her upbringing. Her parents raised the family in the upper-middle-class suburb of Evanston, Illinois, and encouraged debate among their kids. "With my parents it was all about learning," Abbie remembers. "It was all about ideas, and not necessarily about arriving at the right answer. My parents emphasized how to explore something, how to pick it apart from every vantage point." Her mother was a painter who worked in silkscreen, and taught classes in their home. "Our mother introduced us to our minds," Carol told me at her Upper West Side apartment. They made frequent trips to the Art Institute of Chicago, and took advantage of all the cultural resources the city had to offer. "She immersed us in ballet classes, theater, museums, and literature," Carol remembers, although she steered them away from the Girl Scouts, believing the uniforms smacked of fascism. This multifaceted approach plays out today not only in Abbie's teaching—she combines elements of Eastern philosophy, psychoanalysis, and medicine—but in her orientation toward life. "I love music, art, language, dance," Abbie says. "To be an intellect[ual] you take from everything." The family was Jewish, but religion's role in the household was more intellectual than spiritual. Abbie's parents instilled in her "a foundation in Jewish history and leftist politics. I loved the stories of the Old Testament, the epic nature of the narrative," she recalls.

Carol describes Abbie as always being a bit of an iconoclast. "She's always been a badass. She defied our parents, wearing provocative clothes as a teenager," she says. "She even questioned our father at the dinner table in front of guests, a big no-no in our house." Abbie and Carol went to college at Barnard in New York, a learning opportunity that, in Abbie's estimation, "blew the world the fuck open for me!" She adored reading, studying, going to class, and engaging with professors. And she and Carol continued soaking up the city's arts and culture. "We had so much fun. We were culture vultures, going to museums and plays. I remember being happy every second," Abbie says.

At Barnard, Abbie was one of the last students of renowned anthropologist Margaret Mead. (Coincidentally, the concept of syncretism—which states that distinct aspects of different cultures blend together to make something unique and new, and which would become an underlying tenet of Katonah yoga—is foundational in anthropology.)

Her work-study job was to trail Professor Mead with a video camera, documenting her days. Every so often Mead would ask Abbie how she was using anthropology in her own life, and how she enjoyed operating the camera. Mead urged her student to complete her fieldwork by making her own documentary. "And my career was launched," Abbie says.

In 1975, when Abbie was at Barnard, the "boat people" were coming to America from Vietnam. After meeting a group of families who were living in a tenement in Jersey City, she dropped out of school for a year to move into the building's basement and document the refugees' adjustment to life in the United States. The film, *The Phans of Jersey City*, opened at the first Margaret Mead Film Festival, and went on to show at the New Directors/New Films Festival at Lincoln Center, the Montreal World Film Festival, and others. The film earned multiple awards in the documentary category. Abbie was twenty years old.

Around the same time, she got involved in psychoanalysis at the behest of her then boyfriend, a film director ten years her senior. She considered him something of a mentor, somebody who could teach her the skills she was dying to learn. (Seeking mentorship was becoming a theme in her life.) She would devote herself to weekly psychoanalytic sessions for twenty years. "I love the therapeutic process," she says. She urged Carol to study psychoanalysis as well, and the twins teamed up to make films together, bringing analytic principles into their craft. "We understood actors' interiors, and analysis helped us to break down a moment, break down a scene," Carol says. Together, they directed *The Baby-Sitters Club* series for HBO and big-budget commercials for clients that included American Express, Old Spice, Pine-Sol, and pharmaceutical companies. The career emerged organically, but it still took Abbie by surprise. "I always thought I'd be an academic or a rabbi," she says.

In her late twenties, Abbie met the man who would become her husband and they started a family. She found flying all over the country to direct films incompatible with raising three small children. The family moved from the city to the tony suburb of Bedford, New York. But leaving behind her beloved cosmopolitan metropolis wasn't easy: "There were no Jews!" Abbie exclaims. "I was bereft." To fill that gap, she started an extracurricular Hebrew school with nine other families, which also scratched her itch for creativity. She designed innovative exercises such as acting out stories from the Torah, building meditation huts where the kids could learn to develop their spiritual lives, making candles, and singing in a choir. She led the children through their bar and bat mitzvahs and continued instruction until they were sixteen, so that they would have a personal relationship with the Torah.

Abbie found great satisfaction in raising her kids. She was conscientious in instilling the values of communication, confidence, and self-expression in her children, the same values she advances in her classes today. "I am so lucky to have had Abbie Galvin as a mother," her eldest child, Adrian, tells me proudly over the phone from LA, where he's recording music. (He's also a Katonah instructor.) He appreciates her love but also the way she held his feet to the fire, challenging him to find ways to communicate effectively from a young age. "I remember being twelve years old," he tells me, "and I was in a tap-dance class with twenty-five girls. By the third week, I was so upset and couldn't handle it anymore. I told my mom I didn't want to go back." Instead of pulling him from the class, or forcing him to soft-shoe through, she offered him a different option. "She said, 'Fine, you can make this decision yourself, but you have to go talk to the teacher and tell her what you're feeling.' She was big on us learning to communicate, to become real people." When the siblings would get into spats with each other or their cousins, she and Carol taught them how to mediate the conflicts themselves. Abbie also made a concerted effort as a mother to free her children from shame.

When she discovered porn on Adrian's computer when he was thirteen, he remembers her telling him, "It's fine, it's totally natural, everyone does this. I just don't want you to think sex is a naughty thing or something you have to hide." That acceptance of the body, without judgment, is evident in Abbie's yoga teaching as well.

Despite the stimulation of being a mother and a Hebrew school instructor, Abbie craved a tribe of like-minded learners. "I thought I'd find my community at a yoga studio," she explains. She had always enjoyed exercise, and appreciated the way yoga melded the physical, spiritual, and intellectual. Her husband went on the hunt to help her find a studio that would be advanced and esoteric enough to suit her interests. He walked into one close to their home, and met a woman named Nevine Michaan, who was at that very moment teaching his cousin. That seemed like an auspicious sign. "I went that afternoon, and meeting Nevine was like love at first sight, it was a chemical reaction," Abbie says. Nevine became another influential mentor.

At this time, in the early 1990s, Nevine was teaching her particular blended practice at the Katonah Yoga Center, which she founded in 1986. Using principles of geometry, mythology, Taoism, and Chinese medicine, Katonah yoga (named after the town that was home to Nevine's first studio) aims not only to help students build strength and enhance health, but also to lead practitioners to higher insights. Katonah yoga emphasizes theory and visualization, attracting people who want to explore themselves as minds as well as bodies. Nevine and Abbie call their unique blend of yogic philosophy "The Material."

Katonah draws from different lineages of yoga, incorporating the prop use of Iyengar, the poses of Hatha, and the breathing of Kundalini, along with the dualistic ideas of Taoism. By putting oneself in the center of complementary poles like *yin* and *yang*, dark and light, male and female, the intuitive and the scholastic, one finds balance and creates a third thing: you. The idea is to help people develop using the integrity of the yoga poses as a metaphor. How do you develop good boundaries? How do you get over yourself, both in forward fold and as an ego? How do you develop vision, both in looking out from downward dog and toward where you want to go? "You make it about life, not your yoga mat," Abbie tells me.

This teaching through metaphor is very much on display in the class I attend that grim winter day, as Abbie leads her students through the dreaded King of the Mountain pose. As we attempt to keep our arms hoisted above our heads for nine interminable minutes with varying degrees of success (some bring their arms down every half minute to rest), Abbie gives us a tour of our bodies, using a metaphor of the body as a house with ten rooms, each one corresponding to various organs and systems. "Imagine going down to room one," she begins, "your ground zero, your perineum, where you rise. It's your pilot light." She surveys the room. "Bring that pubis forward, Francisco!"

"Then jump up to room two," the tour continues, "back of the head on your right, your attic. Open up the windows and let the bats out. Put a skylight in there. Make it an artist's studio." She goes on like this until we reach room ten, which is ourselves in our entirety, integrating all the different parts of our lives and our potential. "Bring your arms back," Abbie calls out, "so you can be king of your dominion, queen of your ocean."

Picturing the body in this way allows students to imagine the different parts of themselves working together in domestic tranquility, which will hopefully inspire greater harmony beyond The Studio's walls. Katonah yoga sees poses not merely as exercise for the body, but as a way of cultivating the whole organism. As Abbie says, "Change the container, change what's inside."

———

BLENDING DIFFERENT LINEAGES OF yoga to create something unique came quite naturally to Nevine. "I was born in Egypt and came to America when I was little, and because I come from a different culture, I have a different vision," she tells me over a lung-cleansing tea in her current studio in Bedford, New York. Like Abbie, Nevine's interests were vast and diverse. She studied history and religion at Vassar, and began practicing yoga in 1977 at Serenity Yoga, one of the few studios in New York City at the time. "Yoga is like cappuccino," Nevine explains. "In 1970, you couldn't get a cappuccino in New York, just a cuppa joe. Today you can get a cappuccino on every single block. You can get a cappuccino at McDonald's."

Nevine began a daily practice with renowned Hatha yoga teacher Alan Bateman. A few years later, she rented a rabbi's study at the Jewish Center on Eighty-Sixth Street and would drop her daughter off at her mother's so she could teach classes two nights a week. One of her students hailed from China, and introduced her to the Taoist diaspora in Chinatown. She was taken with the philosophy. "The Taoists say the body is a house," she explains. "Make a mess, clean it up. You live in it; it's not a museum. That spoke to me as much as Hatha yoga spoke to me." Nevine saw that by blending these two strands she could create something even more beneficial. And in yoga, there has been a centuries-long tradition of doing just that. "Everybody is trying to get to the same place—joy," Nevine says with a smile. "I teach techniques to get there. I know how to convey esoteric ideas in plain English." Once again, the gift of communication proved essential.

Abbie studied closely under Nevine for five years before taking on her own classes. Nevine remembers Abbie as "a great student and a great learner. She always had a notepad and pen by her mat." Abbie is quick to tell me that the move from her own practice mat to teaching was natural, not something she set out to do. A lifelong student, she saw teaching as a way to learn more. "You have to articulate, hold a room, and understand your own self as you assist others," she explains. Plus, the schedule fit well with her life.

"She understood that not only did yoga have a lot of magic but it was a way of earning a living," Nevine says. (Abbie and Nevine both refer to Katonah yoga as a kind of "practical magic.") "Back then you could teach four mornings a week and still raise your kids."

At forty, Abbie stood in front of her first yoga class. Unlike the majority of teachers today, she never completed formal teacher training. She started out giving instruction in people's homes in the wealthy enclaves of Westchester County and Greenwich, Connecticut, in addition to classes at the Katonah Yoga Center. She steadily developed her goals as a teacher. "I'm always hoping to read the room and make contact with everybody," Abbie explains. "It's my job to know who's late, who's early, who's uncomfortable. I know who's hiding, who's front and center, who needs attention, who doesn't want attention. I have to be the center of that circumference." She credits the intuition she honed as a mother with helping her identify such details.

Her basic aim in teaching Katonah is to help students organize their bodies into structures where their organs can function optimally. Teaching people with a range of proficiencies forced her to find a way to bridge practitioners' gaps: "You have to give enough theory and enough elementary practice for the advanced people to hear the same thing again and not care. The people who really know the practice have heard the same instructions and metaphors ad nauseam." But repetition, Abbie maintains, is a critical part of learning. "You hear something the millionth-and-first time, and you may hear something different," she says.

The finesse with which she tailors her teaching to suit the needs of her students is lucid in her private lessons. One afternoon, two exquisitely preserved women draped in fur and toting lavender Bergdorf Goodman bags came by The Studio for a session with Abbie. They have spent the day shopping, then lunching at the latest Jean-Georges outpost. After changing into stretchy yoga clothes, one of the women makes sure to let it be known that what I am about to see is "not normal! This is half-therapy, half-yoga. We've been doing this for twenty years." Indeed, these two ladies started out taking Abbie's classes in a friend's Greenwich home. Even back then, they say, Abbie had a gift for reading bodies, but they've relished seeing her refine her skills over the years. Abbie moves them into a series of pigeon variations, pressing her feet into their shoulders and down their tailbones. Despite such contortions, the chitchat does not cease. They discuss their children's upcoming theatrical performances, a father's chemo treatment, plans for an upcoming long weekend in Aspen. On the way out, one of the women remarks, "This kind of yoga isn't for everyone. Not everyone wants a knee in their crotch."

Pigeon Pose

Abbie's next private session features no such knees in any crotch whatsoever, as this student, Robin, is suffering from a variety of ailments, including chronic pain and fainting spells. Abbie has her place a blanket over her mat to soften the impact on her knees, a move she typically forbids, as she believes you should be able to feel where your knee is making contact with the ground, uncomfortable though it may be. They start out making small movements, circling their hips on hands and knees. Abbie places two blocks under Robin's hips in a supported bridge. "Next week, we'll get three under there," Abbie says with a smile; the few extra inches of elevation will be a real accomplishment.

She explains her tough love philosophy to Robin with characteristic directness: "When you want to change a river you don't do anything to the water. You change the banks of the river. Talking about your illness won't help. We have to put you in the proper geometry." Robin has already noticed the benefits of working with Abbie. "Two weeks ago, I felt like I was eighty-three," she says. "Now I feel like I'm in my seventies."

BY THE EARLY 2000S, demand for Katonah yoga was growing. Nevine opened the Katonah Yoga Studio in Manhattan's Chelsea neighborhood in 2011. "My goal was to keep the doors open for five years to establish a foothold in the city," Nevine says. During those five years, Abbie's life began to change. Two of her kids were now grown and out of the house, and her divorce was being finalized. Spending more time in the city teaching Katonah classes felt right. She was at the studio seven days a week. Once Nevine reached her goal of five years, she decided she was ready to close the Chelsea studio and head back up to Westchester. But Abbie had gotten a taste of something life-changing: a community dedicated to cultivating their inner lives through the practice of yoga, with her at the center of it. She wanted to stay in the city.

With the help of a Katonah devotee, Sophia Campana, who had a background in finance, Abbie drew up a business plan and began researching potential spaces for her own studio. They looked at dozens before stumbling onto the light-filled, high-ceilinged space in the Bowery. "The wonky staircase leading up to the space reminded me of the ballet studios where I used to dance as a girl," she tells me. Another Katonah student who works as an architect helped with the design. Abbie invested $100,000 of her own money ("my whole life savings," she says) in getting the operation up and running. The Studio opened its doors in August 2016, a real gamble, as New York tends to clear out in late summer. Abbie was a nervous wreck. "I literally paced around my house all night for two weeks when we opened," she says, laughing now. "I knew I wouldn't be able to sleep." By the end of the first month, Sophia reported that class attendance was so robust that The Studio was sustainable. "When I heard that I could sleep again," Abbie says.

Abbie now teaches a dozen classes per week, along with fifteen or so private sessions, not to mention hours spent mentoring junior teachers and crisscrossing the globe giving trainings; she has developed an international cult following. She has been invited to teach in Zurich, London, and Berlin, with hordes of teachers coming from all over Europe to study with her. All her trainings sell out. In one visit to The Studio, I meet Suzanne O'Sullivan, a yoga studio owner from Dublin who has traveled to New York to take group classes and private sessions with Abbie for a week. "I just want to soak up every bit of her knowledge," Suzanne says.

Abbie credits some of her success to becoming a teacher later in life, bringing the whole person she developed over the course of six decades to her instruction. That depth and wealth of knowledge is rare, and is what keeps her students coming back to be around her, not just as a dynamic teacher, but as a kind of sage. As Abbie puts it, "Teaching is about being a person, not about being a yoga teacher, because that's not sustainable. It's not all that interesting if you're just teaching yoga poses. You have to bring everything you are into it." In this way, becoming a yoga teacher is more akin to becoming an artist or a musician: it's a lifelong craft to hone. As an older person, "you have something to reflect on . . . You've lived, you've gone through relationships, had ups and downs. You've already followed a fall and crest of different qualities of waves." You've cultivated wisdom and can draw on a host of experiences, which informs both Abbie's teaching and her understanding of her own practice. "If you're too young," she says, "you might skip over the marination process, the way you develop the material for yourself first. You should develop your own practice, rather than taking classes in order to teach. You only teach classes to enhance your own practice." She very much believes that becoming a teacher is a way to stay a student for life.

Another part of Abbie's charm is that while the ideas she trades in can seem esoteric, she infuses the philosophy with warmth, humor, and irreverence. "She has a boldness that can be missing in the airy-fairy yoga world," Karen Jarman, who participates in a work-study program at The Studio, staffing the front desk in exchange for classes, tells me. "She's pragmatic, and is teaching people tools and practices to be human."

"She's really sassy," agrees one of Abbie's protégées, Studio teacher Alex Sharry. "She doesn't sugarcoat anything."

Jeanette Doherty, a Studio regular and yoga teacher in Brooklyn, loves that "Abbie is so generous with the amount of information she provides. She doesn't hold back to keep you coming. She gives you as much information as you can take."

Emmie Danza, another yoga teacher in Brooklyn, admiringly calls Abbie "just this presence. She knows so much, people worship the ground she walks on." Emmie recalls her first Katonah class with Abbie: "I went with a friend, who told me I was in for a wild ride. Abbie took one look at me and said, 'Hmmm . . .' Before I knew it, she was in front of me with a strap and a foot in my hip, and someone else behind me had their knee in my back, and a dozen people were gathered around watching. I was like 'Holy shit, what is happening right now?!'" That feeling was enough to keep her coming back for more.

4

With her status as a master teacher, Abbie has made her small business viable. But opening a studio is a risky proposition. I learn more about all that this entails from Tangerine Hot Power Yoga studio owner Tamara Behar, who has been studying with Abbie for three years. Her energy is warm and hospitable, and she has a luxurious mane of red hair that she keeps piled high on her head in the heat of her ninety-degree studio. She is fifty years old, "and I say my age proudly," she proclaims.

Tamara is the person who first brings me to The Studio. With her mat next to mine, she patiently helps move my limbs into the correct positions. At one point, in a plow pose, supine on my back with Abbie urging my thighs over my face, I look over at Tamara and whisper that I feel as if I'm being waterboarded by my own obesity. She just laughs, and says (lies) that I'm doing great. "I hate plow too," she confides, "which is why I try to do it every day."

Plow Pose

Like Abbie, Tamara didn't set out as a young person to become a yoga teacher. A graphic designer by training, she enjoyed a twenty-year career in advertising, art directing for blue-chip clients like Revlon and John Frieda. But in 2008, at the height of the recession, she, like many, got laid off. Which was when she decided to plunk down $2,300 from her savings into a two-hundred-hour teacher training at Yoga to the People. She has since completed over thirty trainings of varying lengths.

Studying yoga and how to teach it has helped her reach a deeper and more personal understanding of the practice—and herself. For most of her life, Tamara struggled with eating disorders and exercise addiction. She would spend much of her handsome advertising salary on fitness classes and personal trainers. But after studying with the legendary power yoga innovator Baron Baptiste in 2009, her issues with food began to improve. She steadily developed a dedicated following at Crunch gym and a small studio in Brooklyn for her challenging and introspective Vinyasa flows, designed to raise the heart rate and tone the body in a state of moving meditation. Her sense of playfulness and lack of pretention were a big part of her appeal.

But the ease she exudes in class didn't come naturally. Over smoothies whipped up in her beautiful Downtown Brooklyn apartment, a short walk from Tangerine, she tells me she actually found it very hard at first to stand before a room of strangers and teach. "I just couldn't get the words out," she says. Because of her dyslexia, she would teach from the back of the room, to better call out left and right sides. "It was a form of hiding," she realized, and so she forced herself to build confidence through repetition. It took a full year of teaching until she felt comfortable. She likened the experience to rollerblading when she lived in San Francisco in her twenties: "I would map out my route to avoid the hills because I was afraid. But after a few months of practicing and getting better, I was eventually able to fly down those hills. It's the same with teaching." I found it relieving to hear that even excellent teachers sometimes struggle to find their voices, that not all come out as fully formed as Abbie.

At Tamara's second training in 2009, the instructor asked trainees to close their eyes and imagine themselves five years hence. A vision came to her: she would own her own yoga studio. Five years later, she signed the lease for a gorgeous space in Downtown Brooklyn, a sandalwood-scented and gently lit sanctuary. *Tangerine*, the studio's namesake, means "slightly stronger and sweeter than an orange." That combination of strong and sweet delighted Tamara, and reminded her of a favorite yoga sutra, *sthira sukham asanam*, which translates to "steady and sweet" or "effort and ease." Stumbling upon this definition of *tangerine* was an aha moment: "That's it," she recalls thinking. "It's bright, spirited, and doesn't take itself too seriously. All the things I want to be in life!" The studio feels like a living room, with regulars gathering over juices and coconut water after class, making sure on their way out to nuzzle Tamara's two small dogs, Charlie and Ella, who sit on a towel on the studio's front desk.

On a freezing Saturday morning just before Christmas, her 9 a.m. class is full, as it usually is. Mats are squeezed a few inches from one another, and students in various states of undress to suit the heat of the room are already warming up in their own flows. Tamara taught at other hot studios in Brooklyn before opening Tangerine, and she sees the heat as another prop to help students open up. ("Would you rather practice in a freezer or an oven?" she asks me. "It's that simple.")

"Feel the heat on your skin," Tamara says to the room. "Let it absorb." She plays a short interview of Bono and the Edge, speaking in deep Irish brogues about how joy is the opposite of fear. "Let's feel that joy this morning," she says.

We lie down on our backs and cross our knees one over the other, drawing them into our chests. "This might be hard for some of you," Tamara says. "It's really hard for me. It might be easy for some of you, and we're jealous!" She gives a throaty laugh. Whereas Abbie's particular talent is her attention to fine bodily detail, Tamara's is to disarm the people who walk through her doors. "I teach as I am," she later tells me. "I don't feel the need to use fancy Sanskrit words. I always talk like a real person." But she does use language clearly and creatively to convey the concepts she's teaching. "Breathe! From front to back, from side to side," she implores. As we suffer through a plank, she urges us to refine our vision: "Don't just look out, look WAY out!" I've heard Abbie say a version of this in her classes: that we want to train our gaze out because that's where our future resides. Tamara's translation feels a bit more accessible. She doesn't reference potential future selves waiting in the distance, but she still gets us to look beyond the boundary of our mats. "*THAT'S* it!" she often proclaims with a broad smile when a student drops a shoulder or unclenches a jaw. "I love to see people release," she says.

Today's class is the first for a pair of gentlemen who set up in the back row. They wear baggy basketball shorts and have sweated through their T-shirts before the first downward dog. Even I can see these poor fellows are struggling to put themselves in the most basic of poses; I catch their knees slipping out over their ankles in lunges, a perennial yoga no-no. (Knees should be lined up just above the ankle; otherwise, you can hurt the joint.) But Tamara goes over to them just a few times to correct their form, when she could've just stayed by their mats the entire class. "What's the point of telling them they're a mess? They know they're a mess!" she says. As a teacher, she would rather avoid putting a student on the spot.

The Katonah material in her class is subtler than Abbie's but offers a fresh perspective on the run-of-the-mill Vinyasa power flow, common in metropolitan areas. She discusses organ systems and how our bodies and minds respond to the current season, but does so in plain, direct language. Her gentle hands-on adjustments orient the practitioner back to their center, to show where they are off balance: "You don't need to clench your left butt cheek at all!" she yells to a butt clencher. She leads the class through exercises to open the soles of our feet, and then to a tabletop position with flipped wrists. "Feet and wrists connect to the neck," she explains. "In cold weather, when we are scrunching our necks and wearing boots, it's even more vital to stretch these parts. When we open up the top of the foot, we open up our necks." The echo of one body part in another is straight from Katonah. Abbie would've been proud.

Tamara says she is totally present when she's teaching: "No matter how bad of a day I've had, it all falls away when I walk in that room." But teaching students and owning a studio are two different things, although enterprises that Tamara seems equally well suited for. She brought her aesthetic vision from advertising into designing the space, which was raw when she found it in 2014. "Tamara isn't hippie-dippie patchouli," D. J. Martin, her business partner and principal investor, tells me. "She doesn't come from money. She knows what it's like to work hard and isn't afraid of it." She and D.J. met when a friend of Tamara's asked him to review her business plan. D.J. has been working as an angel investor for start-ups by women for the past fourteen years, providing capital in return for a stake in the company. He took the subway to see the neighborhood where she had identified the commercial space she wanted to rent, and saw construction and new apartment buildings going up. "I saw lots of potential," he says, in the gentrifying neighborhood, but "the space was a concrete slab. It was just cinder blocks, no water, no HVAC, no electricity, a complete shell." Tamara wanted to design a space that felt like home. She insisted on a pristine finish and a Sub-Zero fridge so she could offer juices and coconut water for sale, along with perks like free towels and mats, and a cool lavender-scented hand towel to refresh with at the end of a sweaty class. "I love to offer these as amenities because I have no interest in walking around with my mat and a towel," she says. (She also brings in books and candles from her apartment to lend a lived-in vibe, though they often go missing.) The cost to open after the complete renovation was north of $750,000.

Tamara and D.J. remember the anxiety of opening week, fearing no one would show up. But each class had at least one person, a very promising sign, according to one of the senior yoga teachers they had hired. Two years prior to opening, Tamara had dropped all her Manhattan classes and begun teaching exclusively in Brooklyn, hoping to cultivate a supportive community there. It paid off: When it came time to hire instructors, she knew every single one of them personally. Her devotees from other studios followed her to Tangerine as well.

The studio's growth has been steady since opening in 2015, with class attendance strong and at capacity most weekends. Tamara reports the studio was "cash flow positive" within a year—a good thing, because their monthly expenses are more than $50,000 just to keep the lights on. These expenses include rent, payment to front-desk staff and teachers, and laundry, which alone runs over $4,000 a month. D.J. says he has begun to recoup on his initial buy-in, but "it's a long-tail investment," he tells me. "It's not for the faint of heart, especially being small, not part of a chain. It's a big leap of faith." He and Tamara don't plan on creating franchises like Soul-Cycle or other fitness boutiques; their vision for the studio is something more bespoke and small-scale. But the venture is still not without risk. If the studio fails, D.J. admits, "Tamara can't just go back to her ad job, she's been out of the business too long." A love of yoga or of teaching isn't enough to justify this sort of a mammoth risk; you have to be able to bring a business mind-set to the work.

Being a business owner has its own headaches. As an owner, Tamara hires and mentors her teachers; plans retreats, trainings, and immersions months (sometimes years) in advance; and keeps tabs on the reviews on ClassPass, a subscription fitness service where students can rate their experience at any studio they attend. For any given class, two people might write two completely different reviews. Too hot in the room, one might say; not hot enough, says the other. And then there's the stress of the financial precarity of going all in on a small business. "I have no plan B," Tamara says. Some days she finds herself moving through life one pose at a time.

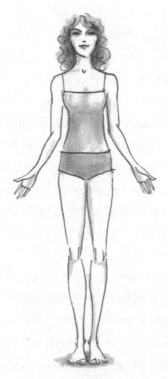

Mountain Pose

5

Abbie Galvin resembles something of an old-fashioned guru for her yoga community, though she is quick to shun the term. "A guru needs a flock, like a priest, for his or her legitimacy," she explains. She sees herself more as a mentor, someone who "encourages students to explore other realms of yoga and of life itself." In the past three years, The Studio has become a destination for teachers who want to bring new zest to their practice. Abbie leads several teacher trainings a year, which take place in the US and Europe and sell out within days. At one point, I ask Studio manager Sophia Campana if people ever become obsessed with Abbie, resulting in stalkers. I mean it as a joke, but it's true that the intense relationship between guru and devotee can sometimes take a dark turn.

For most of yoga's history, a student would have learned the practice via devotion to a guru. He (the vast majority of classical yoga practitioners were male, save ancient lore of female witches, or "yoginis," who gained the strength to fly from feasting on male flesh) would dedicate his life to his teacher, forsaking worldly attachments to live an ascetic and celibate life in a temple, far from his family, society, and distraction.

The figure of the guru is unusual within Western, particularly American, culture. Our national character is based on fierce individualism, an adolescent you-can't-tell-me-what-to-do sneer in the face of authority. What to make, then, of the traditional practice of presenting oneself to an omnipotent guru like an empty cup to be filled? And yet the influence of master teachers from India on the way yoga is practiced in America today cannot be overestimated.

Two of the most luminous yogis in American history were themselves trained by the same guru, enrolling in Sri Tirumalai Krishnamacharya's yoga school in Mysore, India, as classmates of Indra Devi. Krishnamacharya is widely credited with reviving Hatha. The first was B. K. S. Iyengar, who would go on to found Iyengar yoga. The eleventh of thirteen children, Iyengar was born in the midst of the 1918–19 influenza pandemic. Sickly and malnourished, the fifteen-year-old was invited by his brother-in-law Krishnamacharya to move to Mysore to improve his health through studying yoga. Though Iyengar's constitution improved, it came at the expense of respect from his guru. Krishnamacharya didn't think the sickly Iyengar would amount to much of a yogi, and tasked him with mundane household chores. The guru would often withhold food until Iyengar mastered a series of difficult poses. After three years of study, the adolescent Iyengar was allowed to teach all-female classes, because of ideas around the impropriety of full-grown men teaching women. Yoga was still mostly the province of men at the time, but Iyengar believed the practice could benefit everyone—not just cloistered devotees. In 1937, with his guru's blessing, he relocated to Pune, in the western Indian state of Maharashtra, where he taught thousands of pupils, popularizing Hatha yoga on the subcontinent.

He touched down in the United States in 1956 in Ann Arbor, Michigan, where he found his style of yoga resonated with a newly yoga-jonesing American public, as it emphasized exercise, proper alignment, and the body's ability to heal itself. What made Iyengar especially distinct was introducing props, including yoga blocks, straps, and blankets to help the student assume more advanced forms with some assistance. His book *Light on Yoga: The Bible of Modern Yoga* sold millions of copies when it came out in 1966, and is still popular today. There are Iyengar yoga schools in more than 250 cities across the globe, and elements of his teachings can be spotted everywhere. Katonah yoga's ample use of props, for example, owes much to Iyengar. As Holly Hammond of *Yoga Journal* writes, "Nearly every Western teacher has been influenced by his emphasis on anatomical precision, many without even knowing it."

The Vinyasa yoga practiced in many contemporary American studios and gyms also owes much to another of Sri Krishnamacharya's disciples, K. Pattabhi Jois. Jois is synonymous with Ashtanga yoga (meaning "eight limbs" in Sanskrit). Students of Ashtanga yoga are expected to memorize a series of poses and practice on their own without a teacher. One must master one series before being granted permission by their Ashtanga master to advance to the next. The vigorous practice is said to "boil the blood" to remove toxins and render it clean. Jois believed "it is only through sweat that disease leaves the body and purification occurs."[18]

But the most infamous Indian guru to make his reputation in America is Bikram Choudhury. Bikram (first name only, please) reportedly started practicing yoga for sixteen hours a day at the age of four—although this is difficult to verify, as Bikram is prone to hyperbolic claims, such as that he invented the disco ball, launched Michael Jackson's career, and was best friends with Elvis. His guru was Bishnu

Charan Ghosh, a principal founder of the Indian physical culture movement of the early twentieth century. Ghosh was a true yoga celebrity: he would give demonstrations of incredible feats, such as stopping his pulse, allowing an elephant to walk across his chest, and bending a bar of iron with his throat. He set up his own College of Physical Education in Calcutta in 1923, and instituted yoga competitions across India. Bikram won the All-India National Yoga Competition at thirteen years old, and would go on to win the next three years as well.

By the 1970s and '80s, jogging and aerobics were taking off across America, and amateur yogis found themselves craving a more physically demanding practice. Bikram had by then developed a "torture chamber" style of teaching: students would hold the same twenty-six poses and perform the same two breathing exercises (in the same order, taught the same way) for ninety minutes in a room heated to 105 degrees. With the encouragement of actress Shirley MacLaine, Bikram arrived in Los Angeles in 1973 and opened a studio in Beverly Hills that would attract celebrities such as Candice Bergen, Madonna, Barbra Streisand, Michael Jackson, Martin Sheen, Susan Sarandon, and Raquel Welch. His punishing asana sequence helped the stars stay slender for film roles.

Bikram's legacy to American yoga isn't so much in the originality of his poses, or his use of heat (which he has trademarked), but rather that he found a way to franchise. He would do for yoga what McDonald's did for the hamburger: codify, package, and consolidate his product into a comforting uniformity. Bikram proved a master at training teachers in his trademark style and sending them out in the world; at the apex of his success, there were 650 Bikram yoga studios worldwide. He would accomplish this in part by figuring out a way to speed up the teacher-training process.

For centuries, one became a yoga teacher by studying under a guru for years, as Bikram did under Bishnu Ghosh. In more recent history, aspiring Bikram teachers have been sequestered in a hotel conference center for two months, attending classes and lectures twice daily. To say that these sessions were cult-like is an understatement. Wearing the color green was forbidden (Bikram loathes it), and students had to ask permission to go to the bathroom. Schedules and rules kept students deprived of food, water, sleep, and sex. Humiliation was typical and used as a tactic to break down the student's ego. Graduation was incumbent upon memorizing a forty-five-page "dialogue," or script, that must be delivered to the letter without variation. The teacher was to be Bikram's mouthpiece, never demonstrating a pose and never adjusting a student. The goal was simply to say the script, and so to create a facsimile of Bikram himself. In the words of Benjamin Lorr, author of the terrific *Hell-Bent*, an exposé of Bikram teacher training, Bikram "can spread his yoga with no screwups and with completely mediocre teachers." Every three years, teachers are required to recertify. Three hundred eighty devotees attended Bikram's 2010 training in San Diego, earning him nearly $4.15 million from that session alone.

In his seventies, Bikram until recently still led instruction in a black Speedo, owned a fleet of dozens of Bentleys and Rolls-Royces, guzzled Coca-Cola, and chowed down on fast food. That odd charisma, along with his branded series of poses that many insist have changed their lives, drew people in with fervent devotion. But these sometimes-charming eccentricities (and the good Bikram has done for thousands of students) have been overshadowed by the numerous sexual assault charges against him. In 2017 alone, there were six separate lawsuits against him filed by former students in California. The accusations range from racial discrimination to hate speech to rape. Similar to the tactics of predator Harvey Weinstein, Bikram would invite students to his hotel room late at night, demand a massage, and then violate them. Bikram has been ordered to pay a total of $17 million in court rulings, and in November 2017, Bikram Choudhury Inc., filed for bankruptcy. Many studios bearing the Bikram name rebranded to hot yoga.

Before filing for bankruptcy, Bikram was ordered to pay his legal advisor Minakshi "Micki" Jafa-Bodden $6.8 million[19] for firing her when she started investigating claims of assault against him. He failed to pay, and a judge issued a warrant for his arrest. He has since fled the US, and should he return, he will face prison time.

But Bikram is hardly hiding out in obscurity. He still leads teacher trainings in Acapulco, Mexico. The price of his nine-week training is now between $12,500 and $16,600, depending on double or single room occupancy. His website assures students that they will have ample time to purchase Bikram-branded gear from the Bikram Boutique on the hotel premises. The guru still teaches many of the classes and delivers lectures.

Though the case of Bikram Choudhury is egregious not only for his acts of violence but also due to the lack of real consequences he has faced for taking advantage of his position, he is hardly an outlier. The founder of Ashtanga yoga, Sri K. Pattabhi Jois, has been accused by dozens of followers of having touched their genitals as an "adjustment." (Indeed, "accused" seems insufficient a word, as disturbing photographs of Jois adjusting women inappropriately are widely available online.) Swami Satchidananda, who gave the opening invocation at Woodstock, was confronted at a symposium in Virginia in 1991 by a group of protesters who accused him of ongoing sexual abuse. Swami Rama, who in 1969 founded the Himalayan Institute retreat center, had a suit filed against him by a victim who said he sexually assaulted her at age nineteen at his Pennsylvania ashram. He died in 1996, but a jury awarded the plaintiff $2 million in damages the following year. Amrit Desai, one of the earliest pioneers to bring yoga to the West, and who often orated on the virtue of celibacy, confessed to multiple sexual relationships with students at his Kripalu ashram in 1994. The center closed its doors for five years then reopened in 1999 with a new secular mission of advancing the art and science of yoga.

The yoga community, like all industries, is experiencing its own reckoning in the wake of the #MeToo movement. But what is specific to yoga is the guru-disciple relationship, which is based on the student's total surrender and trust. This kind of hierarchy creates a fertile environment for abuse, one we have seen far too many times, from the Catholic Church to competitive gymnastics. When the #MeToo movement hit critical mass in the fall of 2017,

Rachel Brathen, more popularly known as Yoga Girl, received over four hundred stories via direct message from among her 2.1 million Instagram followers, all citing inappropriate and menacing behavior by male yoga teachers.

Yoga Alliance, the organization that oversees yoga teacher training programs, is working to reevaluate its eighteen-year-old teaching standards,[20] and the group's Consent in Yoga initiative is trying to give students more autonomy over their own bodies in class. They have created a wooden poker chip that students can place on the corner of their mats, indicating whether or not they would like hands-on adjustments. These are just the beginning rumbles of what will be an ongoing conversation to ensure yoga studios remain the nurturing spaces they are intended to be.

6

Aspiring yoga teachers today need not cloister them-selves in monastic isolation to hone their skills. Nor should they grant a guru absolute authority. But echoes of the ancient master-student dynamic do still remain.

On a sweltering summer morning, a few hours before Abbie will begin teaching the third day of a thirty-hour Katonah training program at The Studio, she and five apprentices huddle around a table for a meeting. The apprentices are women of all ages and backgrounds, with two commonalities: they have fallen in love with Katonah yoga (and have the toned bodies to prove it) and have committed to a yearlong curriculum under Abbie's tutelage. A couple of them are already certified yoga teachers. Over the course of the year, they will meet with Abbie one-on-one and as a group, complete her weekly reading and reflection assignments that delve into The Material, practice teaching private classes to Katonah's roster of seasoned instructors, support The Studio through housekeeping tasks (like serving snacks during teacher trainings), and eventually teach community classes.

Abbie's is not the only apprentice program in the city, but those offered at other places typically target younger teachers, and many charge upward of several thousand dollars for the privilege of one-on-one mentorship and doing chores around the studio. Abbie's program is free. She finds the idea of "charging people who aren't yet making a living through teaching" unconscionable, and, like the ancient gurus of yoga, she feels a vocation to pass on what she's learned.

This particular morning, Abbie wants to go over the structure of private sessions. All the apprentices will practice giving a one-on-one class to a Studio teacher in the coming weeks. Many people who seek out Katonah yoga for private instruction are in pain or experiencing other bodily trouble—injuries, autoimmune diseases, slow recoveries from long bouts of illness—as The Studio has gained a reputation as "the yoga hospital." Abbie assures her apprentices of how much they can glean from working with people for whom yoga poses are a challenge. As always, she urges her students to see the big picture: "Someone will tell you their shoulder hurts and you'll realize that it's not their shoulder hurting them, it's their life hurting."

The apprentices present case studies they've already encountered while working with, as Abbie calls them, "difficult bodies." Linsey, a young woman who's training to become a doula, sips on a brown smoothie in an enormous Mason jar and talks about running a prenatal session for women who never had an exercise regimen prior to getting pregnant. For this student, even the restorative poses Linsey thought would come easy were a challenge. "She couldn't even lift her hips one inch off the ground to do a supported bridge," she reports. Abbie tells her she should have gotten this client to go on her hands and knees, because anyone can do that. "You don't fix a body from where it's wrong," Abbie counsels. "Show her what she *can* do. Let the right angles of the geometry support her body."

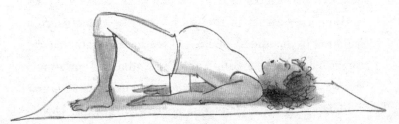

Bridge Pose

Young teachers seem to worry that an instruction like this can sound too basic, but Abbie encourages them to rely on tried-and-true tenets.

Abbie knows just how personally new teachers can take frustrating experiences in the yoga studio, especially if they perceive students as doubting their abilities. Fighting through these insecurities is a challenge for all novice instructors. Teacher Jeanette Doherty recalls how important it was to her when she was starting out that she felt every student in the room liked her: "That's a really hard position to put yourself in, right?" she says, laughing about it today. "Studying with Abbie helped me recognize that it is not my job to get students to like me. My job is to show up with what it is that I have to share, and to share it in the sincerest, best way I know, and to let them experience it without trying to control the outcome."

Even though she has internalized this maxim, her self-confidence still gets tested. She describes teaching a class at Tangerine earlier in the week, where a student started laughing in the middle of class. "I felt for a minute that she might have been laughing at me," she admits. "But even if she was laughing at me, that's not my business." Gaining confidence in the content one is conveying helps. Developing that layer between the personal and the professional makes teaching more sustainable in the long run. But Jeanette still starts to tear up a bit just thinking about that day. "I'm a crier!" she says.

Back at the apprentices' table, the conversation turns to a challenging student in this week's training, which most of the apprentices are attending. One woman in particular has been standoffish and prickly. When Abbie asked the trainees on the first day to go around the room and reveal something about themselves, this individual opted to pass. She later brought up her anxieties around appropriate adjustments, in light of the assaults that have plagued the yoga community. Abbie says that at every training she has ever run, someone will bring up the topic of sexual impropriety. "Frankly, I find it a little ridiculous," she states with her characteristic candor. While Abbie is quick to acknowledge the endemic abuse in the yoga community (perpetrated by "almost every big-shot male teacher, and even a few women," she notes), she wants to move on from the conversation on her watch. "I'm a mother. It's just not going to happen," she says. "But, this student's feeling of insecurity can make everyone feel unsafe," she explains to her apprentices. "You have to acknowledge it, respond, and move on."

Still, Abbie does not condemn where this woman is coming from. "She may be a porcupine, so you have to figure out how to get a porcupine to lower its quills," she continues. When it came time to give the student an adjustment later on in the session, "I didn't adjust her from the front because I knew that would feel too confrontational. Instead, I made an adjustment from the back while she was in reverse namaste. She softened up, felt safe, and smiled."

"You gave her the experience in a way she could receive it," an apprentice surmises.

"Yes, that is your job!" Abbie exclaims.

Abbie and the apprentices go over a writing assignment on the magic square, a philosophical concept within Katonah that grids out the metaphor of the body as house, with corresponding organ systems and how they all interact. Even Abbie admits it's complex and difficult. The session goes over the allotted time by half an hour, so everyone has a chance to read their reflection and receive feedback. She listens intently as each apprentice reads their assignment aloud, totally absorbed in their words. People listen to Abbie with rapt attention because she listens to them just as hard. She offers a rare gift to whomever she is engaging with in the moment: her full and complete attention.

———

BEING A YOGA TEACHER is much more about being a teacher than it is about yoga. An excitement for yoga is a good place to start, but it won't get you far in the long run. Jason Crandell, a senior instructor who has amassed an ecstatic following in the millions from his series of online classes, puts it best. "Loving your yoga practice is actually not that compelling a reason to be a yoga teacher," he tells me over the phone, from his home in San Francisco. "You have to love interacting, communicating, building a methodological structure for people to learn effectively. There are too many teachers who think 'I'm going to get the right yoga clothes and learn hard poses and show how proficient I am and teach classes.' Those things will not earn you an adult living. You have to be an extremely effective communicator."

Abbie echoes Crandell's sentiments: "Having a passion for yoga is great, but being a teacher is a whole different thing." She likens teaching to mentoring: it's about caring deeply for students. But even more crucial than caring is the ability to articulate and make accessible esoteric concerns. "You are trying to find the words that speak to a person implicitly, so that you can move them," Abbie explains. "The best teachers send a core of affirmation to their students so they feel understood, seen, and spoken to. Being a teacher [requires a] capacity to make contact in an intellectual, spiritual, and emotional way that gives someone an experience that is edifying and elevating." That's no small task. Abbie believes this ability is a gift from the divine, but she also thinks it can be developed.

The most common path to becoming a yoga teacher is through an accredited two-hundred-hour program stamped with the approval of Yoga Alliance, the largest worldwide registry for yoga teachers and schools. The move toward greater oversight began in the late 1990s, when a group of older guru-trained yogis gathered to discuss establishing standards for the mushrooming number of teacher training programs that were popping up to meet the growing demand. They coined themselves the Ad Hoc Yoga Alliance, which eventually became Yoga Alliance. The organization helped to weed out shady or subpar programs, a mission that continues today. Graduates of Yoga Alliance–credentialed programs are encouraged to rate the quality of instruction online, where resoundingly poor reviews are enough to get a training program pulled. Beyond creating norms for programs to follow, the organization's emergence also reflects the shift from studying for decades under a guru, as yoga had been taught for centuries, to something a bit more accessible for practitioners of the twenty-first century. Though it now seems inevitable, this was perhaps one of the most momentous shifts in the long history of yogic culture.

Since teacher training is a big investment of time and money, going in with a clear understanding of what you hope to get out of the experience can be useful. Holly Ledbetter, a full-time teacher in Brooklyn, urges prospective trainees to spend a few hours writing and reflecting before taking the plunge. Questions to consider: "Why do I want to care for other people? And why do I want to care for other people in *this* way?" "Having a selfless intention for what you're doing can sustain you," she says. Other students just seek to "deepen their practice," as the ad copy of many a teacher training proclaims. For Emmie Danza, her first teacher training did just that. "I'm a visual learner, so I felt like I got to see the shapes for the first time on other people, in a small group setting," she reports.

Doing your homework and taking time to find the right teacher for you is hugely important. Petra Lee Ghin, a parttime yoga teacher and full-time hair stylist and salon owner, espouses the benefits of research—and not just online. "You should choose at least three or four training programs to visit," she says. "Go to their classes and spend time hanging out in the studio to see if you like their vibe." Petra also remembers feeling a bit overwhelmed trying to learn all the systems of the body during her training. "I wish I would have signed up for an Anatomy 101 class at a community college beforehand," she laments.

One aspect many who take the leap into training don't expect is just how emotionally raw the experience can be. Abbie Galvin and her senior teachers laugh that there is So. Much. Crying. (Other yoga teacher inside jokes include the prevalence of snoring during savasana and the inevitable episode of student flatulence.) Brooke Gassel, a yoga teacher who lives in Rhode Island and works part-time manning the front desk of a spa, speculates that the reason for this out-pouring of emotion isn't because people who seek to deepen their yoga practice are particularly crybabies, but rather be-cause a good teacher training program offers "a safe space to let people practice finding a voice for emotions that may have been otherwise repressed." Training can "normalize and destigmatize mental health issues," she explains, as "over the course of spending several months together, it comes to light that everyone else is suffering just like we are. When we share and communicate, you can feel the healing impact."

The benefits of teacher training go beyond physical and mental health to something almost existential. "It taught me that there was another way to live my life," Brooke tells me. "Before training, I actually didn't believe it was possible to break out of expected job and living situations and to have

more autonomy doing the things I love. Having a community of like-minded people helped support the idea that I
could live unconventionally." She left an unfulfilling nine-
to-five job in New York for a communal-living setup in
Providence, Rhode Island, where the lower rent and cost of
living has allowed her to support herself by teaching yoga
far away from the big-city grind. "I'm in a place that's a hundred times better emotionally and physically even just a year
after taking that training," she acknowledges.

Though all the teachers I spoke with considered their first
two-hundred-hour training a transformative experience,
there has been a great deal of controversy in the yoga community around the sufficiency and proliferation of such
programs in recent years. As a representative from Yoga Alliance stated in a 2016 article in *Yoga Journal*, "The 200-hour
standard essentially created an entire industry."[21] Teacher
trainings have become the financial bread and butter for
many studios, which can charge thousands in tuition. And,
like other professional programs that train pupils for jobs
that offer neither very high pay nor ample employment, such
as an MFA, yoga teacher trainings, when viewed cynically,
function as a bit of a pyramid scheme. The more teachers
there are, the harder it is to find employment and a living
wage.

Beyond the perhaps questionable ethics around the pro-liferation of such programs, some argue that two hundred hours is simply an insufficient pedagogical foundation for teachers who will be caring for people's delicate bodies in challenging geometries. In a viral 2014 blog post, yoga teacher and self-described "thought-leader in the spiritual industrial complex" James Brown excoriated the accredit-ing organization in a piece entitled "Yoga Alliance Is Ru-ining Yoga."[22] He bemoaned the ubiquity of teachers who know little more than how to play a fun soundtrack and do advanced poses such as handstands without understand-ing how to support students through these poses step-by-step. He writes, "Nearly all of these inadequately trained yoga teachers have been educated at or above the minimum standard that is almost universally accepted by those who hire yoga teachers. So, why don't these teachers know how to teach an authentic and safe yoga practice? The problem lies with the body who sets the industry standard for yoga teacher training." Yoga Alliance clapped back,[23] writing, "Mr. Brown is apparently unaware that most yoga teachers and schools don't want a credentialing organization to tell them precisely how to teach yoga, or that it would be impos-sible to forge a consensus in the yoga community about a 'specific curriculum.'" This dustup highlights the challenge in ensuring safety standards when yogic education is delivered in a few weekends rather than over decades of study before a guru, not to mention growing concern over the efficacy of teachers.

Author and lifelong yoga practitioner William J. Broad tapped into this anxiety in a widely shared 2012 *New York Times Magazine* article entitled "How Yoga Can Wreck Your Body,"[24] an excerpt from his book *The Science of Yoga: The Risks and the Rewards*. He argues that despite its sheen of safety, yogic physical therapy is actually quite risky for a population that spends the vast majority of the day hunched over a computer. "Indian practitioners of yoga typically squatted and sat cross-legged in daily life," he writes, "and yoga poses, or asanas, were an outgrowth of these postures. Now urbanites who sit in chairs all day walk into a studio a couple of times a week and strain to twist themselves into ever-more difficult postures despite their lack of flexibility and other physical problems." A crop of inexperienced teachers urging students beyond their limits can lead to injuries. But the danger isn't just in faulty instruction. Broad cites a 1972 article in the *British Medical Journal* by Oxford neurophysiologist W. Ritchie Russell that provided evidence that certain yoga postures, such as hyperflexion of the neck, can cause brain injuries in healthy people. Another paper that came out the following year cited a case study of a twenty-eight-year-old woman who experienced a stroke while in wheel pose, a deep backbend typically completed at the end of class. In 2002, a survey by the Consumer Product Safety Commission documented forty-six emergency room visits due to yoga-related injuries, up from twenty the year before.

Today, in almost any yoga class, you will hear the teacher call out modifications for difficult poses, easier moves to master before rising to a challenge. Teachers like Tangerine's Tamara Behar urge students to practice the poses they may avoid, but to listen to their bodies to arrive at that perfect point where a pose feels difficult but not so strenuous as to be unsafe. This is where a student's self-awareness is crucial, so that they don't push their bodies past their limits.

As a novice teacher, it can be better to err on the side of caution in the poses you demonstrate rather than trying to impress your students with uncomfortable contortions their bodies may not be equipped for. As for students who are concerned about their teachers' classroom experience, most teachers' credentials are easily searchable through the Yoga Alliance website. If safety is a principal concern, it's wise to seek out teachers who have advanced training under their belts beyond the standard two-hundred-hour course.

7

Don't expect your first teacher training to launch you into a glitzy career. Most elite yoga teachers consider a first two-hundred-hour training to be the equivalent of an undergraduate degree. And in a competitive job market, there's no knowing how far that'll get you.

Emmie Danza, a twenty-six-year-old full-time yoga teacher in New York, had just graduated from college when she took her first yoga teacher training at Yoga to the People. Leaving college without any student loans, she considered herself lucky to be able to throw herself into the teaching hustle. Emmie found herself working the front desk at Yoga to the People, making $12 an hour, and earning $35 for each class she taught. She admits that her parents helped support her in these early years.

At a donation-based studio like Yoga to the People, individual teachers are considered less important than the classes they teach, which is why teachers do not choose their own schedules, nor are their names associated with their classes. "It reinforced that it wasn't the Emmie show," Emmie tells me, "which is an interesting way to learn, but it's a fine line. That can be a valuable perspective when learning how to properly be there for students, but it can also hold teachers down and makes you feel as if you don't have an important role there." An upside was that she gained experience teaching giant sixty-person classes.

After completing her basic teacher training, Emmie began cold calling other studios to see if they had any openings. But with little experience and only one studio to vouch for her, she kept getting rejections. "How do you set yourself apart from a million and one yoga teachers?" she wondered. She decided to emphasize her experience caretaking for spaces; she was, after all, working the front desk. If nothing else, she thought, she could help around a studio. After a few months, her luck reversed when she called a brand-new studio, Sweat, with no teachers on their roster yet. She was invited to audition.

The process of auditioning for a teaching position ranges from awkward to nerve-racking. It varies by studio, with some inviting a roomful of prospective teachers to tag-team a class, each doing a three-minute chunk, with the next candidate in line picking up the baton from where the last left off. Some ask the interviewee to teach any part of their sequence for three minutes, to mimic the experience of spying through a peephole on a typical class. Others will have you teach an entire class to the studio manager and another teacher or two. The best scenario, Emmie says, is when an owner or manager takes your class at another studio. "That's far more organic," she says. This is what Tamara Behar did when she interviewed Emmie to come teach at Tangerine Hot Power Yoga. Emmie was honored that her prospective boss would take the time to see her at work in her own environment.

Sweat offered Emmie two 6:45 a.m. classes, which she still teaches alongside her lessons at Tangerine. Back then she got paid $60 per class. Most studios will try to lowball you, she explains, so it's important to ask for more than you're offered—something that can be notoriously difficult for women, which a majority of yoga instructors are. "Hopefully you find a place where they respect you because you're catering to a room full of humans and caring for a space," Emmie adds. After teaching for four years, she now commands $70 as her base rate per class at a standard studio. "Context is a driving force," she explains, when it comes to how much she gets paid. "Corporate jobs versus studio jobs will require a different rate. Same with private clients. There is no one-size-fits-all."

THE RAW ECONOMICS DO not paint a rosy picture. Most studios treat their teachers as independent contractors, requiring them to sock away enough of their paychecks to cover taxes, not to mention other fees. (Getting liability insurance for yoga teachers is a must.) And while Abbie can charge $175 per hour for a seemingly unending supply of private clients, a novice yoga teacher can expect to make perhaps $50 per class, or as little as $15. The figure is shocking, given that a single class can cost a student $15–30. Teacher Jeanette Doherty recalls what Abbie tells her protégées: teaching yoga won't be your primary means of making money, at least not initially. "You might be bartending on the side, you might keep your day job, you might have to have a sugar daddy," Jeanette jokes.

When I asked the dozens of yoga teachers I interviewed what is the single most important thing to consider when thinking about becoming an instructor, the answer was resounding: How are you going to make a living? If yoga is your sole source of income, you may well burn out. "When you focus on making a living as a full-time yoga teacher, you chase experiences like shiny objects," Abbie explains. "You'll teach randomly, and try to fit yourself into whatever the gig is. You'll teach some corporate thing, then a birthday party. And after a while, from chasing the wrong effort, you will diminish yourself."

One of the benefits of pursuing a career in yoga at a later age, as Abbie Galvin and Tamara Behar found, is the added financial security of having a little money saved up from previous employment. Yoga teachers without a nest egg have to hustle. As author, journalist, and certified yoga instructor Emily Gould remarked, "Yoga teachers make freelance writers look lazy."

Take Dan Gottlieb, for example. At six foot seven, he isn't exactly who you'd peg as a sun salutation devotee. He wears a Stetson on his head and Gucci high-tops on his feet. With chunky 1980s spectacles, he looks more like a hip-hop producer than a yoga teacher. He teaches a class at Studio B that combines espresso, foam rolling for sports recovery, and yoga, which he's trademarked as "Sproga." He's also trained the Detroit Pistons in how the subtleties of yoga can enhance their game on the court.

Dan played college basketball and was hoping to continue his career overseas until he was laid up with an injury.

He became addicted to pain medication in his early twenties and dropped out of school. After months of debilitating struggle, he kicked drugs cold turkey, and began looking into alternative and Eastern healing techniques, dabbling in acupuncture, massage, Pilates, and yoga. He pieced together an income however he could, including working as a bouncer at a strip club and staffing the front desk at a yoga studio. Within a year, he took his first teacher training there.

"I took the ten-thousand-hour rule very seriously," he tells me over a plate of fried chicken, referencing Malcolm Gladwell's maxim from *Outliers*: that to become an expert in any field one must devote ten thousand hours of practice. "At one point, I was teaching seventy-two classes a month, subbing for anyone, Monday through Sunday, no days off," he says. He was used to such diligent effort from his basketball days in college, when he would pay a janitor to let him back in the gym to practice on his own after the team cleared out. "You have to say yes in the beginning," he tells me. "You have to sub six a.m. classes. You can't be picky. Studios are going to pay you whatever they are going to pay you until you prove yourself. Once the word is out about you, then you have more leverage." This is where the energy of youth seems to benefit the upstart yoga teacher nicely.

———

MANY TEACHERS THINK OF group classes as an opportunity to hopefully reel in a bigger fish: a private client. The benefit is in the math. A teacher can earn double to triple for an hour of individual instruction versus what she'd make leading a group class for the same amount of time. Gaining as many private clients as one can handle makes the economics work, if you want to support yourself through yoga alone. The downside? More hustle.

Private sessions can take place in a studio like Tangerine, where rates are $150 per hour, with the studio taking forty percent to staff the front desk and provide the space, and the teacher pocketing sixty percent. Many teachers will travel to clients' residences, which means more money, but also more time in transit. New York City yoga teachers adjust their private rates based on how far they have to travel to meet a client, as they can end up spending twice as much time on the subway as teaching.

Client visits can also bring yoga to people who aren't necessarily able to travel to a studio for class. Holly Ledbetter, a woman in her early twenties with short curly hair and an infectious smile, works with private clients who have Parkinson's disease and chronic pain. She got her start teaching

Vinyasa flow at studios and gyms, and then began working with students who have Parkinson's. In addition to teaching traditional classes, Holly focuses on yoga therapy, or working with people whose mobility and health are diminished, homing in on the most restorative parts of yoga practice. The work has been transformative for her clients, and also for her, reframing her beliefs about what our bodies and minds are capable of.

"Yoga is a practice of coming from your mind into your body," she tells me over a pot of rooibos tea, on a morning when the sun has finally surfaced after lying dormant behind the clouds, and the world feels as though it's rejoicing. "When a person's body is the thing that's failing them, it's hard to walk into their apartment and tell them, 'Hey, we're going to focus on this thing that's causing you an incredible amount of pain.'" She has developed techniques of body and breath awareness that help her clients focus on a part of their bodies, even if it's just the fingernail on their left pinky, which is not in pain. "It's about finding moments of pleasure, no matter how small," she says.

More training programs have cropped up in recent years to ensure that teachers have the tools they need to teach students with disabilities. Accessible Yoga's curriculum includes ways to do asanas from a wheelchair or bed, and the

Integral Yoga Institute in San Francisco has begun offering Accessible Teacher Training. Jivana Heyman, the director of teacher training at the institute, told *Yoga Journal* in a 2010 interview that making teacher training accessible to yogis with disabilities offers benefits beyond the purely physical. "There is a tendency for people who are disabled to become the receiver of care and to always be the patient and the student," he said. "Becoming a teacher transforms the way people think of themselves."

Sydney Spears, a licensed clinical social worker in private practice, has taught Hatha, Vinyasa, and Restorative yoga for twelve years. In her first two-hundred-hour teacher training, she remembers asking herself, " 'What happens if I go to adjust a student to the 'correct' position, and I end up triggering them if they are a survivor of abuse?' The answer I got was not satisfactory. The student is supposed to tell the teacher not to make adjustments. Well, the average student isn't going to walk up to the teacher and announce their trauma." That experience got her thinking about how to create a program that was more attuned to students' psychological needs.

As a woman of color in her sixties, Sydney had always been invested in diversity. But the light bulb went off when she learned about a special certificate to work with veterans. Her dad had served in the military, and she realized teaching yoga to veterans would allow her to work with "people who have PTSD, physical limitations, and traumatic brain injuries. This kind of teaching was bringing it all together for me—diversity, respect for people who are often forgotten about, and social justice." She now also teaches survivors of abuse.

The trauma-informed yoga instruction in Sydney's classes draws on evidence-based neuroscience to help practitioners join neural connections that may not have been made in childhood, or reconnect those that have been disrupted due to traumatic experiences, as well as work through the fight-or-flight response of the automatic nervous system. For Sydney, this all starts with creating the safest space possible for her students. The language used to communicate is of utmost importance here. "We call ourselves facilitators, not teachers or instructors," she tells me, and she refers to the asanas as "forms" because words like "position" or "pose" can have negative connotations for survivors of sexual or ritual abuse. Sydney also uses her instructions more as an invitation. Calling out a warrior two form might sound something like this: "If you would like, you are welcome to possibly experiment with this particular form, and one way of doing that would be to bring your arms out to the sides of your body. But know that you can actually lower your arms, which may be more useful to you, or you can bring your arms up to the crown of your head if that's something you'd like to experience in this present moment. Maybe you want to be in stillness right now and that's totally okay." Looking around a typical class of Mindful Warrior yoga at the Kansas City VA, you would see participants standing, sitting in chairs, and some lying on their mats, all doing what feels right to them.

Sydney has witnessed the impact this kind of teaching has had on her students. They will tell her about healthy

Warrior Two Pose

choices they make, like eating more vegetables or drawing on breathing techniques when they find themselves triggered. Some have reported decreasing their medication. Sydney finds this feedback hugely rewarding. "To see them feel like 'I can live again?' It's just amazing," she says. She is now developing a trauma-informed yoga class for veterans with spinal cord injuries.

WITH THOUSANDS OF QUALIFIED yoga teachers out there, making your classes unique becomes imperative. Some teachers accomplish this not by further specialization, but by being fully themselves. Petra Lee Ghin draws on the stories behind the asanas to add psychological depth to her teaching. In a recent class, she told the story of the Lord of the Dance pose, a standing backbend in which the student stands on one foot, clasps the top of the other foot, and leans forward to create a crescent shape in the back, all while maintaining the body's balance. "Instead of just giving cues like 'push your right foot into your right hand,' I can reflect the story of the pose and say 'now you're destroying something from within, something that doesn't serve any purpose,'" she explains. Petra also brings a lot of her personal life into her teaching. "I teach from my own

suffering," she says. "I go into inversions with them, and sometimes I fall. I think that gives students permission to try things out, and to trust me when they see I will humble myself to imperfection right along with them."

Jeanette Doherty structures her classes thematically. A self-proclaimed theater geek, she recently saw the musical *Waitress* on Broadway, and loved the elements of Joseph Campbell's *Hero's Journey* she saw in the production. So she decided to design a series of classes around that famous circuit, including a forearm stand as a "dark night of the soul" asana, since that pose is particularly challenging for her. Like many teachers I spoke with, Jeanette spends a few hours mapping out her sequence and practicing, writing down the flow in a notebook. She will then teach these classes throughout the week. By the time the classes come around, she no longer needs to refer to the notes, since the themes and ideas live inside her body.

Following the Taoist emphasis on the seasons, Abbie Galvin adjusts the poses in her classes based on the time of year. In the winter, she leads her students through grounding poses on the floor "because the winter is all about going down and burrowing in," she explains. The seasonal shifts also correspond to different organs. Winter, for example, is associated with water, so Abbie teaches poses that target the

kidneys, which process the water in our bodies. But Abbie no longer preplans classes as much as she once did. "I see who's in the room, I think about the season, I think about what we need," she says, and goes from there, extemporaneously.

Instructors can allow their personalities to shine through in subtle touches as well. Brooke Gassel always gives students a head and shoulder massage while they rest in savasana. "Just taking a moment to place your hands on a student at the end of class goes a long way in helping them to relax and feel connected to the experience," she says. The choice of music, or lack thereof, can reflect a teacher's vibe. Some instructors will choose to open and close class with a quote to reflect on. All these little choices contribute to curating an individualized, tailored experience.

Others carve out their own space without even stepping foot in a studio. Through YouTube, subscription apps, and personal websites, you can reach millions of people and cultivate a following by creating instructional videos. San Francisco–based teacher Jason Crandell was a pioneer of this strategy. Ten years ago, Jason pitched *Yoga Journal* a series of twenty-minute guided practices for a podcast and a dozen video classes. "They were low-budget and had low production values," he admits, "but it introduced a l

students to what I had to say as a teacher." He never got paid, but the series accumulated millions of hits on YouTube and catapulted him into the public eye.

Three years later, Jason was approached by Derik Mills, the founder of Glo, a leading online education forum where subscribers pay $18 a month for unlimited access to thousands of classes. By this point, Jason was teaching at every major international and domestic yoga conference, publishing frequently in *Yoga Journal*, and traveling thirty times a year to lead workshops overseas. He admired Derik and his business model, which compensated teachers for their work. So he figured he'd give online classes another go.

Jason now has fifty-two thousand followers on Instagram, and *Yoga Journal* has named him "one of the teachers shaping the future." There's no huge difference between teaching online and in real life, he says, other than class length. Most people use home practice to supplement studio practice, so courses range from twenty to forty-five minutes. "These classes aren't lower intensity," he explains, "just shorter duration." And a whole lot of work still goes into preparing them. He tells me "the sequence should be thorough and balanced, with focal points and learning objectives." He likes to mimic the studio experience in his videos, because that's what's most comfortable to him. "I don't practice on a mountaintop or in a rice field," he says.

Jason's videos are so successful because he stays true to his values as a teacher, which are to provide clear and rigorous instruction. His manner is simple, direct, and accessible, free of anything remotely New Agey. He's pitched daily by companies offering him lucrative deals to feature their wares, which he summarily rejects—shocking in the social media economy of sponsored posts. "I'm a yoga teacher, not a salesperson," he says. "I don't think about my brand, or strategic partnerships . . . I create Instagram posts that drive people to content they're going to learn from. That's my focus. I don't think about making posts of me pressing up into a handstand in sexy leggings."

And oh how many sexy leggings there are. In some ways, Instagram has become the bane of many a yoga teacher's existence. "It's so important and it's SO annoying!" one frustrated yoga teacher who wished to remain nameless bemoans. "If I see one more post of a fucking backbend and a corny quote, I'm going to scream!" Like most of what rises to the top on social media, the most popular yoga accounts are of attractive, toned, and often white people photographed in tropical locales, their coconut-oiled abs reflecting the Caribbean sun as they hold a pose impossible for the mere mortals among us, their million-plus followers liking single-handed handstands and other feats that defy gravity and reasonable limits on flexibility. These images can get inside the head of an aspiring yoga teacher, and not in a good way. Teacher Megan Hardwick has to urge herself to remember that these accounts are highly curated, and not reflections of daily life. She relies mainly on word-of-mouth for her own classes, instead of becoming enslaved to creating content.

But as damaging as some of these perceptions can be, social media can also expand society's idea of who can be a yogi. Jessamyn Stanley, a yoga teacher and podcaster based in Durham, North Carolina, is a full-figured African-American woman in her early thirties whose Instagram account boasts 368,000 followers. Her fans double-tap photos of her in the same poses as Instagram celebrities like @beachyogagirl and @nakedyogachick and videos of her practice prove that people of any size can reap the benefits of yoga. Jessamyn is the author of *Every Body Yoga* and has been featured in ad campaigns for Kotex, carving a niche for herself through being authentic.

YOGA RETREATS ARE ANOTHER way to offer something a little different. Patricia Pinto, a stunning, tall, and tan Venezuelan woman with long sun-kissed brown hair, has just returned from leading a dozen yoga disciples on a weeklong surf-and-yoga sojourn in Colombia when I meet her for lunch in Brooklyn. I could've screamed with jealousy. Patricia has been spearheading retreats since 2014, when she founded her company, Love Surf Yoga. A lifelong traveler, she has traipsed to exotic locales all over the globe on a shoestring budget, places as covetable as Tulum, Mexico ("before it was Tulum," she says), and Bali ("before it was Bali"). She grew up surfing in Venezuela and loved the ritual of it most of all. "We'd all meet up early, bring our coffee and breakfast, and go check out the conditions. It always felt so exciting," she recalls. After doing the yoga hustle for five years, with many mornings of waking up at four thirty, and not a Sunday off in all that time, she organized her first retreat to Costa Rica.

With a million and one retreats out there, Patricia wanted to put her particular spin on the project, combining her love of surfing, yoga, and budget travel to create a unique and accessible experience. "These are not luxury retreats for a reason," she says. "I have payment plans. I bring together a group of people with similar mind-sets." A six-day/seven-night retreat to Nicaragua with daily surfing, yoga, and meditation, as well as a single room and all meals included, costs $2,300. A similar itinerary in Colombia costs $1,850.

Patricia likes the low-key vibe. "If someone is paying four thousand for a retreat, it becomes more of a service than an experience," she says. She has taken groups to Barbados, Mexico, and South Africa, supporting the local community wherever she goes. "I always make sure it's locals staffing the hotel and kitchen, not expats," she says.

Organization is the secret to a retreat's success, Patricia says. She arranges everything, including logistics, travel, transfers, hotels, and schedules. She also likes to play with a "juicy theme" for the week. Past retreats have involved Chinese elements, Buddhist meditations, and mudras. But no matter how conscientious the organizer, the unexpected can happen. On the first day of one Costa Rican retreat, a volcano exploded. Half of the still in-transit participants' planes were grounded. Two women were stuck in Miami, where Patricia's sister lives; she arranged for her sister to take in the stranded travelers for the night. But most annoyances that plague people on retreats are more mundane. "People freak out over twisted ankles, they cry because they don't want to share rooms," Patricia reports. How does she attend to the whims of people who are still paying money for a vacation? "I try to make them feel supported, to see what we can do," she says. "My service background comes in well in those cases."

While Patricia's business is sustainable, she's not making a fortune. "I pay myself for each yoga class about what each student would pay to take a studio class," she says. So, about $25 per head per class to teach yoga and meditation overlooking the ocean. There are worse ways to make a living.

But Patricia has worked hard for her career, and without the invisible support many other, younger full-time teachers depend on. "I'm the only person I know who put herself through the yoga world without help," she tells me. "Most people have a partner or family money. There are yoga teachers who teach three times a week. They are beautiful and fabulous, and their husbands are paying their rent." I find her candor refreshing; the economics of being a full-time yoga teacher in a place as expensive as New York City had not been adding up for her.

Teaching somewhere other than New York City has its benefits. Brooke Gassel, who relocated to Providence to give her yoga career a go in a place without exorbitant rents, tells me, "It is wildly more competitive and sceney in New York. You almost don't notice how much effort you're putting in to keeping up with the clothes, the lifestyle, and the fancy poses until you leave." She finds that the students in her classes differ as well, which she enjoys. "The age range is much wider in my classes in Providence," she says. "In

New York, the demographics were mostly twenty- and thirtysomething white women."

But in a place with lower rents, fewer people, and less of a demand for yoga, pay tends to be lower as well. Brooke gets paid a base rate of $15 per class, plus more per head if over ten people. Nancy Curran, who teaches at Yoga on the Beach in Key West, Florida, started out teaching classes at a hotel. There, she made $30 per class even if no one showed up, and $7 a head subsequently. Today, she charges $18 for a drop-in class, compared to an average of $25 to $30 in New York or Los Angeles. But with no overhead (literally: her classes are in the open air), she can pocket all that profit.

IF PATRICIA PINTO IS a bit of an outlier in New York with her self-made trajectory, she is also an outlier in another way: she is a teacher of color. Despite yoga's increasing global popularity, the face of yoga still seems to be thin, white, and female. "There are not a lot of Latina women teaching," Patricia notes. I ask her what she thinks would make yoga more diverse. "I think making it more approachable," she says. "I've noticed that many people who practice yoga, as well as some teachers, are just uber thin. So maybe more diverse teachers?"

Which is how I find myself on a rainy Friday morning making my way to Petra Lee Ghin's nine o'clock yoga class at Red Planet, a Muay Thai boxing studio in Bed-Stuy, Brooklyn. Petra took her first teacher training at age forty-three. She teaches Budokon style, which draws on poses and philosophy from martial arts. Her class is filled with regulars who train in boxing and jujitsu, and have an easy, supportive camaraderie. There are men and women of all shapes and sizes, none of whom are wearing expensive yoga-branded clothing. On a blue-padded floor that smells distinctly of many grappling sessions, Petra leads us through a heart-pumping series of poses that bring out our inner warriors: we thrust imaginary swords at our adversaries, and incorporate roundhouse kicks into the asana flow. She concludes with a meditation on gratitude to ourselves.

After class, I catch up with Sulyn, a fortysomething massage therapist of mixed-race descent and student of Petra's. She has recently started dropping in on the occasional yoga class after a twenty-odd-year hiatus, mainly due to the competitive climate in New York, "where someone is always bumping or jostling you." She practiced Iyengar while dating a woman who taught in the lineage, and dabbled in Yin, a mellow form of yoga, but found it too enervating. She'd wonder, "Should I be sleeping? I can do that at home!"

After the 2016 presidential election, she felt vulnerable as a queer woman of color. "I wanted to feel like I can protect myself," she says. She began training at Red Planet, and discovered Petra's yoga class was a good complement to her regimen of kicking and punching. "I want to move like a ninja," she jokes. And she found Petra's teaching style "very empowering. It's not hokey, like I've found some yoga classes to be." What drew Sulyn to yoga was the hope of strengthening herself physically and mentally in a political climate antagonistic to her identity. And she's seen the results in her body. "I can do a handstand now, occasionally!" she exclaims.

A Trinidadian immigrant of Indian and Chinese descent, Petra tries hard to make her students feel welcome, as she has experienced subtle dismissiveness in many yoga studios. "In trendy Manhattan studios, you only see a certain body type," she says. "Thin girls in bra tops and short shorts. It's not even so much about race, but maybe a certain level of wealth? I won't go to the front in a class like that. I'll go to the back of the room. I feel left out, like I'm not part of the community." She sees her classes as an antidote to this. "I know all my students," she says. "I stay and chat with them." She prides herself on the diversity in her classes, with students from "the gay community, women of color, women and men of different sizes and flexibility." She believes that other studios could attract this kind of diversity by offering more beginner-level classes, manned by experienced teachers who are excited about teaching people foundational skills.

Adriana Adelé, a twenty-nine-year-old African-American yoga teacher in Philadelphia, echoes Petra's sentiments. She's noticed that a studio's vibe can be traced back to its philosophy: "Studios that are rooted in classical philosophy often have the belief that the body is a problem, the body needs to be transcended to reach samadhi, or oneness. It can feed into a very Western mind-set of improvement at all costs." For her teacher training, she chose a studio with a Tantric philosophy, which is more focused on embodiment as a positive. "If you come from the place of your body is a gift," she says, then "coming from a place of diversity is something to be celebrated." Before giving lessons at a new studio, she always asks what philosophy they espouse, to get a sense of the attitude and clientele she might encounter. The answer isn't always enlightening, though. "A lot of times when I ask about the studio's philosophy a manager will just be like 'Yoga!'" she says, laughing.

As a yoga student and teacher of color in an overwhelmingly white industry, Adriana says she has certainly had uncomfortable exchanges. She began practicing when she was "slinging coffee in Oakland in my early twenties," and even in that liberal enclave, there were often only one or two students of color in class. As an instructor, she says, "there have definitely been times when I will get a look from a student like, 'Oh, *you're* the teacher?' I've kind of built up a wall, behind which I try to focus my energy elsewhere when those things happen." Like Petra, she values diversity in her classes, and is careful to eschew tokenism: "The questions I always ask myself when I look out into a room when I'm teaching are 'Does everyone look the same? Who is not here, and why?'"

One pragmatic fix is to teach in spaces that aren't yoga studios. "It can be intimidating to walk into a boutique studio where everyone is in Lululemon," Adriana acknowledges. "Last night I taught in the basement of the public library. People did yoga in their shoes. I told them they were welcome to take them off, but if not, that's cool too! When we recognize that yoga doesn't have to look a certain way, we can let go of those rules." She sees digital platforms as another way to increase accessibility, and credits content creators like Dana Falsetti, who started her own online platform, Practice with Dana, where students can name their price for unlimited access to her videos. All her videos are closed-captioned, signaling that she is trying to reach deaf students, a demographic often overlooked in brick-and-mortar studios.

In many cities, all-people-of-color yoga meet-ups and classes are gaining popularity. And despite the banal ubiquity of yoga Instagram accounts, Adriana appreciates that students can use social media to find teachers with whom they resonate. "There are a lot of yoga teachers of color out there," she says. "It just might take a little more digging to find them." Many of Adriana's students have found her through her handle @adrianaadele, where she posts pictures and videos of her Namaslay workshops, a playful flow to the sounds of hip-hop and R & B.

8

———

Teacher burnout is a principal cause of careers going bust, sometimes even before they've gotten off the ground. Planning classes, traveling, and being completely present for one's students—not to mention coping with financial and existential anxiety—require enormous stores of energy. Emmie Danza believes the reason so many yoga teachers are or were actors or dancers is because holding the attention of a room is simpatico with performing. But that kind of performance can leave a lot of people depleted. "It takes a particular type of person to not let teaching draw everything out of you," she says. "I'm naturally more of an introvert and teaching brought me out of my shell. But I have to recharge." Knowing how to replenish oneself is key to longevity in the field.

Holly Ledbetter recalls feeling annihilated after her first few months of teaching full-time. "I didn't yet have the skills to be incredibly present for anywhere from two to forty people each day, and know how to turn that off when I got home and be present for myself," she says. She caught a nasty flu that persisted for weeks that first winter of teaching. Abbie insists teachers stay home when they're not well—"When you are sick, your body and spirit are not supporting each other, so there is no way you can support others"—but for cash-strapped novice instructors, this can be easier said than done. Holly had to learn the hard way to practice preventative self-care to stave off maladies, both physical and emotional. Today, her repertoire includes time alone, getting a massage, and taking a yoga class rather than teaching one. "It's so easy to get out of balance, and then before you know it you have a sinus infection," she notes.

Practicing all the healthy habits teachers espouse to their students is also a big deal. Good nutrition is critical to fuel oneself during long days of teaching multiple classes and private clients. Patricia Pinto tells me that on long teaching days she avoids sugar and carbs; proteins and veggies keep her going. And as with any profession, time off is important. This is the first year since Emmie Danza began teaching full-time three years ago that she will take a proper vacation, and she was sure to schedule it for August, when the demand for hot yoga ebbs.

The physical tax caught up even with Abbie, who seems preternaturally energetic, by winter's end. She had been traveling overseas and to California practically back-to-back, along with teaching her typical roster of classes and private clients. In late February she caught the flu, which had her laid up for almost a week. "She just crashed," her twin sister, Carol, says. For Abbie's disciples, this display of mere mortality was troubling. One of her students emailed Carol to ask if she was flipped out about her sister. "They see her as superhuman," Carol observes. "That's not good for them, and it's not good for Abbie. She's got foibles and challenges like anybody else."

In spite of the toll teaching yoga can take physically and emotionally, all the instructors I spoke with say the payoff far outweighs the drain. Patricia Pinto calls yoga "a healing method that has proven itself to my students—and myself— effective over and over. I believe that we all need this, and I feel lucky I can make a living doing it." Emmie Danza finds herself sustained by her students. "It's all about coming together with others," she says. "Having the ability to connect with so many people in a mindful and powerful way is where I find the fuel to keep going. It's a gift and I never forget it." And Tamara Behar relishes seeing her students grow and transform. One Tangerine regular recently quit drinking and lost sixty pounds sweating it out at the studio. Tamara received a card over the holidays that read, *I can't thank you enough. I had a really hard year, and this studio carried me through.* She tells me with tears in her eyes: "When you hear those kinds of stories, it's all worth it."

THE BEST WAY TO build longevity into a yoga career is more yoga, and more study. Maintaining a personal yoga practice is critical to staying in the teaching game. Many teachers I spoke with said they would find themselves sacrificing their own regimen of classes and home practice in the first years of teaching to take on another private client or to sub. But one's home practice should be sacrosanct time to connect with and strengthen the body, preventing burnout in teaching and in life in general. As Abbie tells teachers during trainings, "If you don't have a home practice, it's impossible to change as a teacher. And I mean having a home in your own body, the practice of going inside and developing an interior life. Because that is where you will get insights. If you can't go in well, you won't be able to go out well." Enrolling in more teacher trainings can also help you get reinspired by master instructors, who will remind you why you liked this whole yoga thing in the first place. Plus, further practice benefits one's students.

ABBIE STILL FEELS AS if she has a lot to learn. She wants to learn another language and how to play an instrument. She wants to learn how to let go of her omnipresent anxieties as a small-business owner. "I still worry people won't come," she says. "I still have those feelings." The irony as she says this, of course, is the noise of dozens of devotees setting up to learn from her just beyond the door. More than anything, she worries about getting fresh material, new information she can pass on to her students. She has plans to travel to Taiwan for a week to study with a master Taoist. "I just want to keep learning," she says.

Learning, like teaching, to Abbie isn't about being a dutiful student, or manipulating a body to arrange limbs in a picture-perfect asana. When she teaches yoga, she says, "It's not about just picking apart a student's pose. It's about making contact." When she says this, I think what she means is that a good yoga teacher—or teacher of any stripe, for that matter—makes a student feel safe, seen, supported. Heard. So rarely in life do we ever feel truly recognized. A teacher can give a student that gift. It's a gift that transcends any of the asanas or the Material. It's about two human beings coming together in a room and sharing a moment, sharing an experience. "That is really your job as a teacher, to make someone feel understood," Abbie says. "They can change their own pose."

One day Abbie lets me sit in on a Katonah training, where thirty-odd yoga teachers have paid $950 to learn from the master for a week. I ask her what she hoped these student-teachers would take away from the experience. "I hope they get a real understanding of how to use their practice with more imagination," she answers. "They are very competent teachers. But they've been taught the *doing* of the practice. When they look at a body, I want them not to just pick apart the pose. I'd like them to have more theory, more ideas, to be able to read bodies and see more deeply."

The teachers have squished their mats together to face the center of the room, where Abbie sits cross-legged in a pale pink T-shirt tucked into cropped yoga pants that re-semble trousers more than leggings. She kicks off with a metaphor to bring home the point of all of this. "If you're a sea captain and you encounter a storm and you have no skills, that's going to be scary," she says. The room titters. "But if you're a sea captain and you encounter a storm and you have skills, then navigating through it is going to be a fun challenge."

The training does not lack for metaphors, particularly about the magic square. But Abbie also offers a more personal metaphor that drives home a principal tenet, not only of the way she wants her practitioners to approach yoga, but also how she wants them to live their lives. It's a precept that is far too often swallowed up when one makes one's passion into one's career.

"I really love to play piano," she tells us. "And I'm not very good at it. When I divorced my lovely husband and moved out of our big house into a two-bedroom apartment, I gave up my piano. So I don't practice very much. But when I do, I do it with gusto, and I just listen to the music. It's not about being good, or dutiful." She pauses for emphasis. This is the most serious I've ever seen her when speaking to her students, her gravity underscoring how important this belief is to her whole philosophy. "*Wu wei* isn't knowing how to ride a bike and hoping you don't fall," she says, referring to the Taoist principle of "non-action," or "without effort." "It's about how you get to your destination. Knowing the vocation isn't as interesting as really using it."

For all her talk of precision and right angles, what Abbie really seeks to convey is the magic in imperfection, and the transcendence that can come from throwing oneself into trying for the love of discovery, the love of process, divorced from the material outcome. Everything else—the students, the retreats, and yes, even the career—can come secondarily. The goal is tapping into joy.

FORMS OF YOGA

Vinyasa Yoga:
Also known as power yoga, a fast-paced fluid flow designed to get the blood pumping.

Hatha Yoga:
The foundation of Vinyasa and power flows, Hatha tends to hold poses a bit longer and emphasizes stretching.

Yin Yoga:
A restorative practice that balances out the "yang," or fire energy, of Vinyasa and other more vigorous forms of yoga.

Katonah Yoga:
A syncretic yoga practice developed by Nevine Michaan that fuses Hatha with Taoist theory, geometry, mythology, and metaphor.

Iyengar Yoga:

A subset of Hatha yoga that pays special attention to precision and detail; founded by master teacher B. K. S. Iyengar.

Ashtanga Yoga:

A form of Vinyasa that follows a prescribed sequence, developed by Sri K. Pattabhi Jois.

Kundalini Yoga:

A blend of physical and spiritual practices that emphasizes breathwork to unlock latent energy.

Tantra Yoga:

A type of yoga that explores the universe through the microcosm of the human form. Though you won't often encounter a "Tantra studio" as such, it is more of a philosophical foundation for other forms of yoga, such as Vinyasa.

Bikram Yoga:

A trademarked type of Hatha yoga, performed in an unwavering set of twenty-six poses and two breathing exercises, practiced in a hot room.

FURTHER READING

Hell-Bent: Obsession, Pain, and the Search for Something Like Transcendence in Competitive Yoga, by Benjamin Lorr

The Subtle Body: The Story of Yoga in America, by Stefanie Syman

Yoga Body: The Origins of Modern Posture Practice, by Mark Singleton

Yoga in Practice, edited by David Gordon White

Every Body Yoga: Let Go of Fear, Get on the Mat, Love Your Body, by Jessamyn Stanley

Yoga as Origami: Themes from Katonah Yoga, by Kat Villain

NOTES

1 *Yoga Journal*, "2016 Yoga in America Study," https://www
.yogajournal.com/page/yogainamericastudy.

2 Tasha Eichenseher, "Is 200 Hours Enough to Teach
Yoga?" *Yoga Journal*, October 12, 2016, https://www
.yogajournal.com/teach/200-hours-enough-teach-yoga.

3 David Gordon White, *Yoga in Practice* (Princeton, NJ:
Princeton University Press, 2012), 167.

4 Mark Singleton, *Yoga Body: The Origins of Modern Posture
Practice* (New York: Oxford University Press, 2010).

5 Stefanie Syman, *The Subtle Body: The Story of Yoga in
America* (New York: Farrar, Straus and Giroux, 2010).

6 "'Sisters and Brothers of America': Full Text of Swami
Vivekananda's Historic Speech in 1893," *DNAIndia*,
https://www.dnaindia.com/india/report-telling-the
-world-about-hinduism-full-text-of-swami-vivekananda-s
-historic-speech-in-1893-2164870.

7   "This Day in History (11-September-1893): Swami
    Vivekananda Presented Hinduism at Chicago's
    Parliament of the World's Religions," *This Day in History*,
    September 11, 2015, https://mukundsathe
    .com/2015/09/11/this-day-in-history-11-sep-1893
    -swami-vivekananda-represented-hinduism-at-chicagos
    -parliament-of-the-worlds-religions/.

8   "Swami Vivekananda," *Wikipedia*, https://en.wikipedia
    .org/wiki/Swami_Vivekananda#First_visit_to_the_West
    _(1893%E2%80%9397).

9   Mark Singleton, *Yoga Body: The Origins of Modern Posture
    Practice* (New York: Oxford University Press, 2010), 71.

10 Stefanie Syman, *The Subtle Body: The Story of Yoga in
    America* (New York: Farrar, Straus and Giroux, 2010), 71.

11 Stefanie Syman, *The Subtle Body: The Story of Yoga in
    America* (New York: Farrar, Straus and Giroux, 2010), 76.

12 Mark Singleton, *Yoga Body: The Origins of Modern Posture
    Practice* (New York: Oxford University Press, 2010), 92.

13 "Indra Devi: A Pioneer for Women in Yoga," *Zoom Dune*,
    https://zoomdune.com/indra-devi-a-pioneer-for-women
    -in-yoga/.

14 Swami Prabhavananda, https://en.wikipedia.org/wiki
    /Swami_Prabhavananda.

15 Holly Hammond, "Yoga Pioneers: How Yoga Came to America," *Yoga Journal*, August 29, 2007, https://www.yogajournal.com/yoga-101/yogas-trip-america.

16 Stefanie Syman, *The Subtle Body: The Story of Yoga in America* (New York: Farrar, Straus and Giroux, 2010), 234.

17 Stefanie Syman, *The Subtle Body: The Story of Yoga in America* (New York: Farrar, Straus and Giroux, 2010), 234.

18 Sharath Jois, "The Practice," *Sharathjois*, https://sharathjois.com/the-practice/.

19 Kate Fagan, "Bikram Yoga's Moral Dilemma," espnW.com; May 23, 2018, http://www.xgames.com/espnw/culture/feature/article/23539292/after-serious-allegations-founder-bikram-yoga-practitioners-crossroads.

20 David Lipsius, "Standards Review Project," YogaAlliance.org, September 1, 2017, https://www.yogaalliance.org/About_Yoga/Article_Archive/Standards_Review_Project.

21 Tasha Eichenseher, "Is 200 Hours Enough to Teach Yoga?" *Yoga Journal*, October 12, 2016, https://www.yogajournal.com/teach/200-hours-enough-teach-yoga.

22 James Brown, "Yoga Alliance Is Ruining Yoga," AmericanYogaSchool.com, https://americanyoga.school/yoga-alliance-ruining-yoga/.

23 "A Response to James Brown and American Yoga School Blog Post," YogaAlliance.com, January 9, 2014, https://www.yogaalliance.org/Home/A_Response_to_James_Brown.

24 William J. Broad, "How Yoga Can Wreck Your Body," *New York Times Magazine*, January 5, 2012, https://www.nytimes.com/2012/01/08/magazine/how-yoga-can-wreck-your-body.html.

ABOUT THE AUTHOR

Elizabeth Greenwood teaches creative nonfiction at Columbia University. She is the author of *Playing Dead: A Journey Through the World of Death Fraud*.